Endorsements

If your heart is longing for deeper intimacy with God and for breakthrough in your relationship with him, I highly recommend Gretchen Rodriguez's new forty-day devotional. Each day of devotions will take you deeper. I have known Gretchen for many years and can attest to her intense, passionate, and focused pursuit of the Lord.

Patricia King
Author, Minister, Television Host
www.patriciaking.com

Fasting can be challenging as well as beautiful. During this time, we draw closer to Jesus and experience just how much we need him. Gretchen Rodriguez has written a beautiful forty-day devotional. As she says, "This is about Jesus." You will find *The Encounter* to be a wonderful handbook to help you both spiritually and physically during your times of fasting.

Beni Johnson
Bethel Church
Author, *The Happy Intercessor*, *Healthy and Free*, and *The Power of Communion*

Many people have felt the pull of the Spirit toward a season of fasting, and yet they haven't always been obedient to follow through on that divine instruction because they just didn't really know *where* or *how* to start. Maybe you've found yourself in that place. I am so glad that my friend Gretchen Rodriguez has written this timely devotional. It gives you the *where* and the *how*, along with spiritual encouragement, steps for transformation, and Scripture that will speak directly to your heart as you seek an encounter with the God of glory through forty days of fasting with Jesus. Through fasting, we're able to hear the voice of the Spirit clearly and enjoy the supernatural realities of the glory realm. I will be using this devotional myself, and I would highly encourage you to join me in this pursuit. Every moment in the presence of God is a moment of transformation. Are you ready for *The Encounter*?

Joshua Mills
Bestselling Author, *Power Portals:*
Awaken Your Connection to the Spirit Realm
Founder, International Glory, Palm Springs, CA
www.joshuamills.com

THE *Encounter*

40 Days of Fasting with Jesus

GRETCHEN RODRIGUEZ

BroadStreet
PUBLISHING

BroadStreet Publishing® Group, LLC
Savage, Minnesota, USA
BroadStreetPublishing.com

The Encounter: 40 Days of Fasting with Jesus

978-1-4245-6217-6 (faux)
978-1-4245-6218-3 (e-book)

Stock or custom editions of BroadStreet Publishing titles may be purchased in bulk for educational, business, ministry, fundraising, or sales promotional use. For information, please email orders@broadstreetpublishing.com.

Typesetting by Kjell Garborg | garborgdesign.com
Design by Chris Garborg | garborgdesign.com

Printed in China
21 22 23 24 25 5 4 3 2 1

Contents

Foreword

After being a Christian for two decades, I decided to fast. My first fast was for three days, and then I bumped it up to ten days. Eventually, I completed four forty-day fasts, and three of them were water-only fasts. I quickly discovered the atomic power of fasting mingled with prayer. Immediately I felt my spiritual eyes open to a deeper realm in Christ. Yes, it is difficult, and yes, I got very hungry. In fact, my wife once busted me watching the cooking channel on day thirty-nine during one of my fasts. I think I was so hungry I just wanted to look at food and remember what it would taste like. Ha! We still get a laugh over that. But truly, fasting brings the soul into the chamber room of the King, where we learn the ways of God through our emptiness and need.

Fasting is all throughout the Bible. The three greatest men of the Bible each fasted in the desert for forty days: Moses, Elijah, and our Lord Jesus. It should be no surprise that the three most anointed, powerful people to walk the earth each endured forty days without food. As the ultimate test of faith, these biblical greats used their fasts to achieve specific goals. Moses proved his loyalty to God and received the Ten Commandments. Elijah gained instruction on how to lead the people of Israel. And Jesus thwarted Satan's temptations. In each case, they passed their tests and gained new insights into God's ultimate plans.

Throughout church history, some of the great spiritual fathers, godly men and women who accomplished many great things for God's kingdom, have testified to the necessity of prayer with fasting.

For example, John Wesley shook the world for God during the Great Awakening. His fasting and prayer resulted in seeing the Methodist Church rise toward the end of the eighteenth century. He so strongly believed in the power of fasting and prayer that he urged early Methodists to fast every Wednesday and Friday. In fact, he refused to ordain anyone in Methodism unless they agreed to do it.

Other great Christian leaders who made prayer with fasting a part of their lives include

- Martin Luther
- John Calvin
- John Knox
- Jonathan Edwards
- Matthew Henry
- Charles Finney
- Andrew Murray
- And many more

Today, fasting for the believer involves three basic goals: receiving power and grace for ministry, transformation of the heart, and intimacy with Christ. Our fast is to draw close to God and hear his voice. I call it the "Bridal Fast," for we are fasting to become intimate with our Bridegroom Jesus Christ.

Some may be slow to fast, thinking that is simply a "work of the flesh." But the Bible teaches us that we are to engage in good works, such as caring for the poor, helping the broken, financially supporting the work of God, interceding for others through prayer, and fasting. Jesus did not say, *"If you fast"* but *"When you fast"* (Matthew 6:16). Fasting is not a "work," it is a "grace." I have discovered that there is a grace that comes to the one who seeks the Lord in prayer and fasting. It is a grace to overcome the physical longing for food and replace it with a spiritual longing for intimacy with Jesus.

I love how Gretchen Rodriguez has given us such delightful truths to ponder as we fast and pray. She is an anointed lover of God who writes from the overflow of a heart on fire. You will feel the passion on each page. God is calling for people to set apart their devotion exclusively to him. Distractions may nag at you, but Jesus' sweet voice will win your heart as you take the journey into fasting and prayer. I know you will love this book. Expect great things from God as you dive in. Grace and peace be yours, through our Lord Jesus Christ.

Brian Simmons
The Passion Translation Project

INTRODUCTION:

Let the Encounter Begin

When a friend suggested I write a devotional for seasons of fasting, it settled effortlessly upon my heart. As I prayed into the idea, the Lord confirmed his desire for a fasting devotional that facilitated holy intimacy with him.

This particular fast is an expression of our intense desire for more of the Lord. It's a form of surrender that declares that God alone satisfies the deepest cravings of our starving souls. It is our response to his invitation to a lifestyle of holy intimacy and daily encounter. We are setting aside time to be with the One we love.

Jesus is the focus of this fast, not our prayer requests. Regardless of how important our prayers are, we need him more. He is the center around which everything in life flows harmoniously. When we're in sync with him, he imparts faith, strength, peace, and wisdom. When we have him, we have the answers to everything we need. In him, we find life's greatest treasures, so *in him* is where we must stay—wrapped in the reality of God's presence. He *is* our breakthrough. What an incredible privilege it is to honor the Lord not only with words but also with actions. Jesus is worth every ounce of our searching, seeking, and yielding.

Fasting denies the natural appetite, and though you may feel physically weaker, your spirit is growing stronger. Don't be afraid of the physical discomfort. Acknowledge it. Feel the stabbing pain of hunger and notice the weakness of your flesh—they serve as powerful reminders of our frailty and absolute need for God's strength.

When you have thoughts of food, turn your attention to the Lord. If possible, sit for a few minutes with your eyes closed and lean into his presence. Invite his awakening breath to blow upon your life. If you hear a Bible verse, get an idea, or simply feel his love for you, don't dismiss it. Write down everything you sense his Spirit saying or impressing upon your spirit. If you're working or doing something where you can't step away to spend time with him, simply whisper his name in the quiet of your heart. Notice the warmth of his Spirit and his response to your statement of love. He is there with you—now and always.

Fasting often stirs emotions and causes attitudes and unhealthy reactions to rise to the surface. You may get triggered more quickly than usual. This is a great thing. It's a way the Lord uses fasting to reveal the areas that aren't completely surrendered to him or that need healing. Again, I encourage you not to ignore these feelings but to press into his presence and process these issues with him.

During your fast, slow your pace. Step away from distractions like social media, cell phones, news, television, etc., and spend this time with the Lord. Schedule moments for stillness and contemplation where you're not saying anything but simply beholding him in the quiet of your heart and listening. Give yourself permission to stop thinking, to be fully present with the Lord instead of wholly consumed by problems. An overwhelmed mind has trouble hearing the voice of God. Stillness allows the Lord to fill places overgrown with weeds of stress and anxiety with his glory. The anxiety will lift, his glory will become more noticeable, and you may feel lighter and more peaceful. This is the place where prayers are answered. When your mind and soul are at rest, it's much easier to recognize his voice and receive his instructions.

This devotional can be used for any length or type of fasting. Each devotion contains a short encouragement, a prayer, steps for transformation, and verses to ponder. At the end of the book, there is an invitation to close the fast with prayer and holy communion.

It is my prayer that you will encounter the Lord in new and glorious ways.

Gretchen Rodriguez

DAY 1

Him Alone

God is the fulfillment of every promise. All that we desire—breakthrough, wisdom, healing, etc.—has its home in him. He is constant. He is the Sustainer. The profound power we'll find nowhere else. His presence contains our breakthrough, and when we find absolute contentment in him, the most unexpected blessings manifest. Let's not approach this fast as a way to get something from God but as a way to experience more of the One who encompasses all we need. With uninhibited devotion, let's turn our focus to him throughout the day and surrender everything that hinders this holy relationship.

This time of fasting and all that he's working within you will bear fruit for eternity. By setting aside distractions and passionately pursuing the Lord, you're declaring your utter dependence upon him. You've set your heart on a journey of discovery because you want to know him. You long to hear the sweetness of his voice, see the beauty of his face, and experience the safety of his arms. He alone is what you need. When you seek him with all of your heart, you will find him. He wants to manifest his love to you in ways you never knew were possible.

Today's Prayer

Father, I long to know you more. You are the very core of this fast, the reason I've set myself aside. When my soul is in agreement with you and your glory fills my vision, every earthly desire fades. If I had riches, fame, joy, and peace all around, I would still need you, still feel this emptiness that only you can fill. Nothing in this world could satisfy my deepest yearning—to be one with you. So I stand in the mystery of divine encounter with the One who loved me before I drew a single breath.

As I seek your face, manifest your love to me. I want to behold you, to experience you in a way that transforms me and frees me from lowly thinking. Make my desires your desires. Let your holiness infuse my thoughts, emotions, and actions. I want to know you, to live in agreement with what is on your heart, and to pray your words with confidence. Unveil my eyes to see beyond what is in front of me into the limitless possibilities of heaven's plan. As I unite my heart to yours, entirely resigned to your will, you will lead me. You will teach me to pray. You will inspire me to love.

Steps for Transformation

- One of the most important aspects of fasting is spending time with the Lord. If you haven't already, decide on a time of day that you can dedicate to him. I think there's something special about mornings. Starting each day by feasting on his love helps center your attention on the things of God and sets the tone for the day. Regardless of when you decide to be with him, carve out as much time as possible. Release expectations of what you think it will be like and simply enjoy the Lord by worshiping, listening, dancing, reading, or however else he may lead.

- In today's devotion, we discussed the importance of setting aside distractions to focus on him. Pay attention to the time-stealers in your life. A fifteen-minute social media check, a short game on an app, a television show—none of these are wrong—but during this fast, notice these mindless habits. Perhaps you can cut some of them out, and instead, tune into the Lord, ponder a verse, or pray in the Spirit. Learning to be more intentional with the minutes and hours you have and using them to focus on him is one way to grow closer to the Lord.

> *So I stand in the mystery of divine encounter*
> *with the One who loved me before I drew a single breath.*

Scripture to Ponder

Here's the one thing I crave from Yahweh,
the one thing I seek above all else:
I want to live with him every moment in his house,
beholding the marvelous beauty of Yahweh,
filled with awe, delighting in his glory and grace.
I want to contemplate in his temple.

PSALM 27:4

Just as I moved past them, I encountered him.
I found the one I adore!
I caught him and fastened myself to him,
refusing to be feeble in my heart again.
Now I'll bring him back to the temple within
where I was given new birth—
into my innermost parts, the place of my conceiving.

SONG OF SONGS 3:4

Seek more of his strength! Seek more of him!
Let's always be seeking the light of his face.

PSALM 105:4

DAY 2

Fully Yours

There is something beautiful about times of fasting. This physical expression of our internal desire for connection with God awakens every part of us—spirit, soul, and body. As we respond to the beckoning of his Spirit to push aside the plate, a deeper hunger eventually takes over. We become aware of our physical emptiness. We slow down to recognize his invitation to a more fulfilling life.

Fasting forces us to pay attention. It strips away distraction and reminds us of what's essential. Our weak flesh serves as a reminder—every breath and each beat of our heart are dependent on a source more significant than food. For our prayers to flow in agreement with God's will, we first surrender. We resign ourselves to the discomfort of hunger, instead of fighting it. We plunge into the emptiness and discover his Spirit filling every void. We find the One our soul truly loves and deeply longs for. When we didn't realize how lifeless, stagnant, and distracted we were, God, in his mercy, invites us to taste and see that he is good. His presence brings us back to life and restores our soul.

Today's Prayer

Lord, setting aside all distractions, I turn my heart to you. This fast reflects my desire to be fully yours. Make me tender. Capture my attention and teach me to set my gaze on what is true, holy, and magnificent. Draw me close. Even closer, until every yearning for you is uninterrupted.

Though there are situations and people on my heart and my list of prayers is long, I seek you first. I choose to drink from the well of truth so it will saturate every thought and drown every fear. I lay my burdens at your feet as an offering of love, as a token of my decision to trust. I need you. I need your anointing of grace—not just for this fast but every day and every moment.

You're calling me higher. I hear you. Feel you in my bones. This is why I've come: to learn to exist in the reality of your presence, to rise above lowly thinking and soar on clouds of faith, to forsake worldly distraction and run with you—to walk in the peace that defies circumstances. Consume me with the awareness of your love. May nothing hinder me from a lifestyle of holy and absolute devotion.

Steps for Transformation

- We've read about the importance of setting time aside to be with the Lord every day. Another aspect of becoming heavenly minded is to cultivate an ongoing awareness of him. This doesn't mean we're always praying about something specific. Setting our affection on God is simply a posture of the heart. It is a gentle and internal consciousness of him, even while we're busy. I like to compare the feeling of this awareness to a hug. Think of what it's like to be hugged by someone you love. It's difficult to describe the impression it leaves on us, but most people have experienced it. Even after the physical contact has stopped, the warmth and tenderness of a meaningful hug linger. This is what it's like to feel the Lord's presence continually. Let this image settle upon you today, and carry it in your heart as a reference.

- Ask the Father to fine-tune you to the frequency of his love so you can experience this ongoing awareness. Don't feel guilty when your mind wanders. Simply return your thoughts to the Lord. By his grace, it will become more natural until his presence becomes your ongoing experience.

> *Draw me close. Even closer, until every yearning for your presence is uninterrupted.*

Scripture to Ponder

Awake, O north wind! Awake, O south wind!
Breathe on my garden with your Spirit-Wind.
Stir up the sweet spice of your life within me.
Spare nothing as you make me your fruitful garden.

SONG OF SONGS 4:16

Are you weary, carrying a heavy burden? Come to me. I will refresh
your life, for I am your oasis. Simply join your life with mine. Learn
my ways and you'll discover that I'm gentle, humble, easy to please.
You will find refreshment and rest in me. For all that I require of
you will be pleasant and easy to bear.

MATTHEW 11:28–30

Keep your thoughts continually fixed on all that is authentic and
real, honorable and admirable, beautiful and respectful, pure
and holy, merciful and kind. And fasten your thoughts on every
glorious work of God, praising him always. Put into practice the
example of all that you have heard from me or seen in my life and
the God of peace will be with you in all things.

PHILIPPIANS 4:8–9

DAY 3

Search Me

Sometimes we struggle to know how to pray for the situation we're facing or the specific breakthrough we desire. We need to hear from God, but often the emotions or weightiness of our trial sidetracks us. When confusion, frustration, or doublemindedness sets in, we no longer have the clarity of the Spirit. This is where fasting comes in. It serves as an instrument of grace, allowing us to see the mindsets that have prolonged our breakthrough.

When we invite the Lord to examine us, we're declaring our desire for an unhindered relationship with him. Becoming vulnerable with the Lord enables us to face our issues and ultimately demolishes shame. It opens us up to freedom in a way we seldom realize is available until we've embraced it. His faithful response of acceptance encourages us to remain vulnerable. Nothing is hidden from him, yet he loves us just the same. By opening every facet of our being to his searching gaze and becoming comfortable in that place, we stop focusing on ourselves. We lift our heads and hearts in his direction because we aren't concerned about hiding any longer. When we recognize our nakedness before him, it's easier to hear his direction.

Lord, my heart is before you. Search me. Every hidden thought is open to your penetrating gaze. Come with the fires of zealous love that burned before the world began and purify me. You paid the ultimate price to have me without reservation, and I will not deny you. Let the beauty of whole-hearted surrender define me so the ways of man do not.

As I yield everything to you, I'm empowered to pray your will. The desires of my heart are purified in the safety of your presence. Here, you peel away the layers of unbelief that have skewed my vision and limited my faith. Suddenly, I see things from your perspective, and I know that you are the God who always comes to my rescue. Your faithful love is setting me free from anxiety and fear. I feel them falling away—like I'm shedding a cumbersome, restrictive shell. Courage is rising within me as I embrace your cleansing love. You are infusing me with confidence, not in myself or what I can muster the faith for, but in the absolute assurance of your love for me. You are the God of holy resolve. You are the One who leads me and teaches me to pray.

Steps for Transformation

- Something that may happen during this fast, or once it ends, is that the Holy Spirit will shine his light on a specific area of your life that he knows you're ready to change. It's important not to brush off his sometimes subtle nudges. If you're noticing tendencies, stresses, reactions, or thoughts that aren't in alignment with God's ways, acknowledge them, ask him to forgive you, and then release each care to him. Ask him to show you what it looks like to live with the opposite emotion, mindset, or outlook. If you ask the Lord to show you a healthy response, thought process, or way of looking at your situation, he will.

- Recognize that God's power is the only thing that can transform you. Having a fully surrendered heart means you rely entirely on his grace to enable you to change. Instead of feeling heavy or sad about the areas that you need to grow in, praise him. Turn your attention to the greatness of his love for you and rejoice in his faithfulness to help you grow.

> *Come with the fires of zealous love that burned before the world began and purify me.*

Scripture to Ponder

God, I invite your searching gaze into my heart.
Examine me through and through;
find out everything that may be hidden within me.
Put me to the test and sift through all my anxious cares.

PSALM 139:23

Let me describe him:
he is graceful as a gazelle,
swift as a wild stag.
Now he comes closer,
even to the places where I hide.
He gazes into my soul,
peering through the portal
as he blossoms within my heart.

SONG OF SONGS 2:9

There is not one person who can hide their thoughts from God,
for nothing that we do remains a secret, and nothing created is
concealed, but everything is exposed and defenseless before his
eyes, to whom we must render an account.

HEBREWS 4:13

DAY 4

Finding Peace

Our flesh and our spirit often walk in contradiction. We say we trust God, yet inside we're burdened and fearful. Then we hear the call to fasting, and though we want to run and fix everything that feels out of sorts, we accept God's invitation. We position our souls before the Lord and, in humility, release every overwhelming concern. Fasting becomes a posture of stillness and trust. We notice our need for God to take over, and we choose to relinquish our need for control. We yield ourselves—spirit, soul, and body.

One prominent and immediate result of fasting is that it causes us to slow down. It turns down the volume down of nagging thoughts so we can tune in to God. It is here in the stillness of his presence that peace becomes our new normal. From this place of connection with him, the overwhelming circumstances of life lose their grip. Fear, doubt, and unbelief bow to the courage rising within us. Anxiety begins to melt away. The swirling mental chaos slows, and soon we find that we can think clearly again. Peace and trust walk hand-in-hand in an environment of absolute surrender to the Lord.

Father, I dedicate myself to you today. My mind has been bombarded with thoughts of everything but you. But I'm here now, confessing my need to be still and know that you are God. I repent for allowing the cares of life to suck me in. It's not my responsibility to take care of everything. I don't have to worry and continuously think about what's wrong to prove that my concerns are valid. You are greater than anything I will ever face. Your love and faithfulness will be my meditation.

Instead of striving to find the solution to my problems, I devote myself to a lifetime pursuit of knowing you. That's the real goal of this fast—to be one with you and to embrace the beauty of a fully surrendered heart. Here in the place of your presence, I release my life into your trustworthy hands and receive the gift of peace. And when I walk in this peace, all fear, anxiety, and frustration are swallowed in its victory. In the stillness, I find what I need. In the atmosphere of peace, I encounter you waiting for me. Waiting to love me into wholeness. In the calm wonder of faith, I find myself again.

Steps for Transformation

- Having a fully surrendered heart is a choice. By an act of our will, we resign our lives to the Lord, knowing he cares about everything that concerns us. However, unless he shows us where we're not completely trusting him, we won't know what needs to be offered. If something in today's devotion caused a slight "ouch," he was probably highlighting something that you haven't entrusted to him. We discussed finding peace by relinquishing the need for control. Control, which is rooted in fear, is seen by the way we reason, worry, or try to fix everything and everyone. Take a moment and reread the sections of today's devotion that spoke to you and ask him for the grace to let go and trust him completely.

- Pay attention to what you're thinking about. So much of what runs through our heads is contrary to God. You do not have to be a victim of your thoughts. Ask him to bring the unrighteous thoughts to the forefront so you can submit them to him. Then search his Word for the truths that replace the lies you've believed. This is how you capture every thought (see 2 Corinthians 10:5).

> *That's the real goal of this fast—*
> *to be one with you and to embrace*
> *the beauty of a fully surrendered heart.*

Scripture to Ponder

Surrender your anxiety.
Be still and realize that I am God.
I am God above all the nations,
and I am exalted throughout the whole earth.

PSALM 46:10

I leave the gift of peace with you—my peace. Not the kind of fragile
peace given by the world, but my perfect peace. Don't yield to fear
or be troubled in your hearts—instead, be courageous!

JOHN 14:27

Pour out all your worries and stress upon him and leave them there,
for he always tenderly cares for you.

1 PETER 5:7

DAY 5

Thankfulness Precedes the Miracle

When we fast, God often highlights areas that inhibit our spiritual growth. Complaining is one of those stumbling blocks. When we center our attention on what we don't have, it weighs us down. We become cynical and short-tempered. Soon, we grow spiritually and emotionally sluggish and have a hard time agreeing with God. It's tough to believe for the miraculous if negativity has become our default.

A beautiful way to align ourselves with God is by developing the habit of thankfulness. When Jesus wanted to feed the multitude, he took what wasn't enough and thanked the Father. He didn't complain or say something religious like, "I know this isn't enough, Father, but I'm trusting you to come through." He simply thanked God for what he had and then behaved as if it were enough. Thankfulness preceded the miracle.

Let's walk away from this fast with a powerful key to a joy-filled life. At first, we may have to put some effort into finding things to be thankful for. But the more we practice gratitude, the easier it becomes. Soon, gratefulness overtakes us, and our whispers of despair turn to shouts of praise. Thankfulness is the catalyst to some of our most significant breakthroughs.

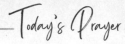

Today's Prayer

Father, thank you for encouraging me to do this fast. I know you're speaking and revealing truths for me to implement. You're reminding me of things I may already know, but I graciously humble myself to receive your instruction. Forgive me for growing accustomed to your blessings without giving you the praise you deserve. I'm sorry for magnifying what isn't going right when there are plenty of things to be thankful for. I want to lavish you with endless thanks and bless you with cries of unending devotion.

I won't wait until everything is exactly the way I want before developing a habit of thanksgiving. I'm going to start today. And in the seasons when it feels like nothing is going right, I will count my blessings and sing your praise. In my mess, you're teaching me, refining me like gold, and imparting grace, which I will one day share with others. Every trial is an opportunity to know you more intimately. It's a chance to strengthen myself by remembering that you are with me and for me. You're doing a work in me that creates integrity, character, and strength. As I fasten my heart to yours, you make me beautiful. May my tears of thankfulness become a gift of worship.

Steps for Transformation

- A practical way to change a negative mindset is to find things you're thankful for. One idea that you may find both helpful and fun is to create a list of things that make you happy. Start a new journal or simply use the Notes app on your cell phone. Can you find one hundred things to put on the list today? Write down everything that gives you a sense of joy and peace or makes you feel thankful. Once you get started, you may be surprised at how quickly you think of things to write. You may even want to continue adding a couple of items to your list each day and watch it grow. When you're intentionally searching for what makes you happy, thankful, or peaceful, it automatically lifts your mood and ignites a heart of praise.

- Your list can run the gamut from small things, like a cool breeze on a hot day or the smell of fresh-cut grass, to very personal and meaningful things about people you love. It can be silly or serious. The point is to write down anything that gives you a sense of contentment or joy.

> *May my tears of thankfulness*
> *become a gift of worship.*

Scripture to Ponder

After everyone was seated, Jesus took the five loaves and two fish,
and gazing into the heavenly realm he gave thanks for the food.
Then, in the presence of his disciples, he broke off pieces of bread
and fish, and kept giving more to each disciple to give to the crowd.
It was multiplying before their eyes!

LUKE 9:15–16

In the midst of everything be always giving thanks,
for this is God's perfect plan for you in Christ Jesus.

1 THESSALONIANS 5:18

Lord! I'm bursting with joy over what you've done for me!
My lips are full of perpetual praise.

PSALM 34:1

DAY 6

Praying in the Spirit

There are many times when we feel the emotion of a trial or situation so intensely that we don't know how to pray. We may spend most of our day consumed with thoughts of what's happening and therefore experience very little peace. And when we set ourselves to pray for whatever is weighing heavily upon us, we spend more time crying out in desperation than in declaring God's truth. We mentally assess our situation when what we need is the Lord's discernment. We need his perspective.

God has offered us a high place in the safety of his Spirit, where we can see the truth from his vantage point. It's up to us to acknowledge our weakness and surrender to the Holy Spirit's wisdom. When we lay down our battleplan and instead pray in the Spirit from the posture of reliance, we glean strength from the One within. We gain insight that comes only from God. We're able to intercede according to his perfect will, which infuses us with faith. Let's tap into this magnificent gift, yield our limited understanding, and admit that he knows the best way to pray.

Today's Prayer

Father, forgive me for acting as if the burden to pray is solely on me and not something we face together. At times I've prayed what I believed was your will without actually seeking your counsel, diving into your Word, or asking your Spirit to lead. Forgive me for the times I've run ahead as if I've already heard your heart on the matter. I confess that at times I find it easier to spin my wheels and work myself into a frenzy of so-called faith because I'm too anxious to lean back into your arms and seek your heart.

Right now, I inhale the peace of your presence and exhale stress. I take up the gift of faith that is seasoned by my trust in you and your love for me. I refuse to obligate myself to a yoke of false responsibility. You are in me, around me, and able to pray with power and perfect wisdom through me. Lord, give me the grace to release these worries that have saddled my soul. Help me to tap into the flow of your Spirit. Pray your perfect will through me now as I thrust myself before you in wholehearted dependence.

Steps for Transformation

- Tapping into the flow of the Spirit in total dependence means you're willing to hear what the Lord has to say, even if it's not what your flesh wants to hear. If you are facing a big decision and aren't sure which way the Lord is leading, I encourage you to sit quietly in his presence. Hold your desire before the Lord with loose hands and an open heart and wait. Refuse to make emotional decisions and maintain this attitude until you are absolutely sure of God's direction.

- Sometimes the Lord answers by sparking a random idea in our hearts, and it settles so effortlessly, we know it's him. Have you experienced a thought or idea landing with such power and peace that it not only surprises you but also completely turns things around for your good? Peace is a significant indicator of the Lord's leading. Think about times you've moved into something without peace. What felt different, deep down, compared to when you knew you were walking in God's will? It's essential to learn from your experiences, so be a good steward and keep track of decisions, why you made them, and the varying levels of peace you've felt.

> *Father, forgive me for acting as if*
> *the burden to pray is solely on me*
> *and not something we face together.*

Scripture to Ponder

In a similar way, the Holy Spirit takes hold of us in our human frailty to empower us in our weakness. For example, at times we don't even know how to pray, or know the best things to ask for. But the Holy Spirit rises up within us to super-intercede on our behalf, pleading to God with emotional sighs too deep for words.

ROMANS 8:26

You, my delightfully loved friends, constantly and progressively build yourselves up on the foundation of your most holy faith by praying every moment in the Spirit.

JUDE 20

Don't be pulled in different directions or worried about a thing. Be saturated in prayer throughout each day, offering your faith-filled requests before God with overflowing gratitude. Tell him every detail of your life, then God's wonderful peace that transcends human understanding, will guard your heart and mind through Jesus Christ.

PHILIPPIANS 4:6–7

DAY 7

Feasting on God

Nothing is more satisfying or fulfilling to our spirits than when we feast upon the Lord's love, presence, and revelation. Fasting is a powerful way to detox ourselves from fleshly indulgences. As we empty ourselves of distraction and feel the discomfort of hunger, we learn that indulging in thoughts of worry or stress is like eating spiritual junk food. Our spiritual hunger is awakened, and we crave the nutrition that our souls truly need—God.

In the flesh's weakened state, it becomes gloriously aware of its dependence upon the Lord. When we're tempted to quit the fast but instead cry out in humility for God's grace, we taste and see that he is good. We're able to feast on his presence in a new way. Suddenly, we understand the importance of a God-focused lifestyle. We begin to find clarity of heart when we're weak, slow, and humbly resigned to God's will. Fasting is a way of declaring our desire to be centered, balanced, and in tune with him, instead of thrown around by the abstract distractions swirling in our minds. Willingly stripped down to the bare necessities of life, we discover that the beautiful One has become our delight.

Today's Prayer

Father, I humble myself before you and ask for the grace to sustain me in this fast. When hunger tries to steal my attention, help me to find strength in your presence. I desire a closer walk with you more than I crave my necessary food. You are my life, my source, and my sustenance. As I feast upon your love, awaken my heart. Increase my longing to know you. Fine-tune me so I hear you more clearly. Cleanse me from anything that would hinder our relationship. Let our connection be the foundation for all I do, think, and pray.

As I grow closer to you, transform my life. I want to be single-minded and fully surrendered to you in ways I've never been before. Decrease my appetite for the foolish gratifications of this world. May I not feed upon the opinions of others but nourish myself in your holy truth. Establish my identity. Clothe me in your glory as I cast aside garments of self-sufficiency and tainted motives such as people-pleasing. Teach me who I am in you so I can pray with confident assurance. May my longing for you, not my appetites for temporary pleasures, guide my life. I want to be driven by a pure and holy hunger to know you.

Steps for Transformation

- What has been difficult for you during this fast? Physical weakness, cravings, not wanting to pray, feeling irritable or impatient—these are all normal aspects of fasting. If we aren't aware that it's common to want to quit, we may succumb to the temptation. But if we use the manifestations and weaknesses of our flesh to remind us of our need for the Lord, they can turn into great blessings. I encourage you to write down the reactions you've had that you aren't happy with. Then discuss each one with the Lord and ask him to reveal what he's teaching you. Let the temptations of the flesh catapult you straight into his arms.

- Also, be mindful of your emotions. They present significant opportunities for growth. Fasting often pushes to the surface unhealthy emotions that we have been ignoring or suppressing. If you're feeling sad or angry, tuck yourself away with the Lord and allow yourself time to embrace and release the emotion. Then, ask the Holy Spirit to show you the root and to heal the wounds, insecurities, and fears. If these feelings are coming to the surface, it means it's time for healing. What a blessing!

> *May my longing for you,*
> *not my appetites for temporary pleasures,*
> *guide my life.*

Scripture to Ponder

You're only truly happy when you walk in total integrity,
walking in the light of God's Word.
What joy overwhelms everyone who keeps the ways of God,
those who seek him as their heart's passion!
They'll never do what's wrong
but will always choose the paths of the Lord.

PSALM 119:1–3

Who is this one?
She arises out of her desert, clinging to her beloved.
When I awakened you under the apple tree,
as you were feasting upon me,
I awakened your innermost being with the travail of birth
as you longed for more of me.

SONGS OF SONGS 8:5

Drink deeply of the pleasures of this God.
Experience for yourself the joyous mercies he gives
to all who turn to hide themselves in him.

PSALM 34:8

DAY 8

Listen

One of the highest privileges of being a child of God, other than our gift of eternal life, is the invitation to know his heart. He is alive, in love with his children, and continually speaking. Matthew 4:4 says, "True life is found in every word that constantly goes forth from God's mouth." This means that he hasn't stopped speaking, and he wants to talk to us.

Two-way communication is a vital part of a healthy relationship with him. And an important key to communication is listening. Unfortunately, many of us spend the majority of our prayer time talking. We run into his open arms, and instead of drawing from the wisdom of the omniscient, all-knowing, almighty God, we vent. There is nothing wrong with pouring out our emotions and telling him our needs. It's healthy to do so. However, we've grown accustomed to doing most of the talking. We rarely listen. Maybe it's because listening means finding stillness, and stillness can be uncomfortable if we're not used to it. There's no better time to connect with the Lord's heart than during a fast. I encourage you to find time to be still and listen today.

Father, forgive me for doing all of the talking. At times I ramble on and on as if you don't already know what's on my heart. Sometimes I need to vent, but pouring out my heart isn't as important as knowing yours. I want to sense your Spirit guiding me as I go about my day. I long to see your will unveiled in my dreams. I believe that your ability to speak is greater than my inability to hear.

In your presence, when I'm still and listening, it's easier to hear your voice and receive your wisdom. The bliss of your presence and the sweetness of your whispers are all the motivation I need to make listening time a priority. This fast is reminding me that I was created for the unfathomable depths of holy intimacy with you.

Lord, pour out your glory. Unclog my spiritual ears and fine-tune me so I flow in unison with you. I long to know the secrets you've hidden for me to find. Lead me on this lifetime pursuit of knowing you. I still myself now in your holy presence.

Speak to me. I'm listening.

Steps for Transformation

- Contemplation, or the prayer of silence, is a beautiful and powerful way to spend time with God. If you're unfamiliar with this form of prayer, it is simply taking time to listen to the Lord without uttering a word. It is a way to honor him by waiting and prioritizing what he has to say. One easy way to begin is with a time of worship. It isn't necessary, of course, but I've found worshiping the Lord through music always brings an immediate awareness of his presence. Once you sense his nearness, turn the music off and sit comfortably or lie in his presence and listen. This is not the time to talk but to hear what he wants to share.

- Notice the words, images, or Bible passages that come to you. Look to see what God wants to show you. Don't try to make anything happen. Simply behold him in a posture of love. If your thoughts distract you, don't be discouraged. When your mind has been busy, and it isn't used to silence, it may take practice to quiet it. Don't give up! Contemplation is one of the clearest ways to hear God and enter peace.

> *Sometimes I need to vent,*
> *but pouring out my heart isn't*
> *as important as knowing yours.*

Scripture to Ponder

Train your heart to listen when I speak
and open your spirit wide to expand your discernment. ...
Yes, cry out for comprehension and intercede for insight.
For if you keep seeking it like a man would seek for sterling silver,
searching in hidden places for cherished treasure,
then you will discover the fear of the Lord
and find the true knowledge of God.

PROVERBS 2:2–5

I'll listen carefully for your voice
and wait to hear whatever you say.
Let me hear your promise of peace—
the message every one of your godly lovers longs to hear.
Don't let us in our ignorance turn back from following you.

PSALM 85:8

When you turn to the right or turn to the left, you will hear his
voice behind you to guide you, saying, "This is the right path;
follow it."

ISAIAH 30:21

DAY 9

When God Takes Over

Many of us fast when we feel stuck. We know God is the only answer to our most significant and seemingly impossible situations. By prayer, fasting, and focused intention, we turn off our minds so we can find his solution. Answers to prayer don't manifest because of our works. But when we humble ourselves through prayer and fasting, we become more sensitive to his Spirit and can more easily hear his direction. When we lay every burden at his feet and take our hands off (surrendering worry, fear, frustration, doubt, etc.), God can finally step in and take over. He can speak to us and show us how to partner with him in a way that brings heaven to earth.

Very often, our need to understand and control our circumstances hinders the very thing we believe for. We fight and try to force a victory with our minds, instead of settling into him and resigning to peace. Here in this place of peace, the God of mercy and grace instructs us. Corrects us. Shows us to pray in accordance with his will. When we come with open hearts, revelation and understanding unfold. As we let go and fully resign ourselves to him, we actually become empowered by faith.

Today's Prayer

Father, I need you. I feel like I'm stuck in quicksand, sinking into a pit of bewilderment. There is nothing I can do to change this. I know because in my might, I've tried many times. Forgive me for striving to do what only you can do. Facedown before you in this dark night of the soul, I surrender. I remind myself that you are good. You are faithful. You love me. You alone are the answer to every prayer. Your very name is power and majesty —delivering me from the power of the enemy. As I draw near to you, you peel away the layers of unbelief that I didn't know were there. Suddenly, I can breathe again.

Releasing control to your reliable hands is the only way for me to come into alignment with you. When I trust you to take over, you whisper words of love that enflame my being and soothe my soul. The presence of peace consumes every fear. Here, I remember that you are good. Now that I'm not striving to fix everything, I can believe. I can hear you again. I see your desire for this situation and understand my part. Faith has quelled the raging storm within me.

Steps for Transformation

- If there are situations that have been weighing heavily upon your heart, it's time to release them to the Lord. Either you can be in charge of your life and live under a weight you weren't meant to carry or you can lay your worries at his feet as an offering of love. Perhaps you've surrendered these difficult circumstances many times before. That's okay. Today the Lord is bringing them back up because he wants you to be free. Releasing control is painful to the flesh, but in the end, it yields the fruit of unimaginable peace. And this position of trust invites his miracle-working power.

- If you notice fear, anxiety, reasoning, or other worldly thoughts creeping back in after you've handed him your cares, don't ignore them. Pray something along these lines: *Father, forgive me for picking these things up again. You know what's on my heart, so I hand everything back to you. I will not focus on the problems. I will focus on you, and you will lead me. You are in control, you love me, and you're working on my behalf.*

> *Now that I'm not striving to fix everything, I can believe.*
> *Faith has quelled the raging storm within me.*

Scripture to Ponder

Trust in the Lord completely,
and do not rely on your own opinions.
With all your heart rely on him to guide you,
and he will lead you in every decision you make.
Become intimate with him in whatever you do,
and he will lead you wherever you go.

PROVERBS 3:5–6

Do not yield to fear, for I am always near.
Never turn your gaze from me, for I am your faithful God.
I will infuse you with my strength
and help you in every situation.
I will hold you firmly with my victorious right hand.

ISAIAH 41:10

The sense and reason of the flesh is death, but the mind-set
controlled by the Spirit finds life and peace.

ROMANS 8:6

DAY 10

A Quiet Mind

We frequently go into times of prayer with firm determination to see the Lord answer our request. But while God loves to answer prayer, he knows we usually need something besides what we're praying for. We need peace. We desperately need the kind of settling peace that grounds us. God often leads us to fast because he wants to get to the root of fear. We think that if our trial goes away, so will our anxiety. That may be true, but God wants to teach us the way of peace that defies trials.

When we fast, our pace slows. Even if we feel more energetic and experience higher mental acuity, we usually notice a sense of inner solace we didn't have before. When we relax into this sort of hollowness that fasting carves out for us, we become detangled from overthinking. It's as if we unconsciously realize that the effort we spend stressing isn't worth it. Once we get to this point in our fast, our inner world gets quieter. We become centered and calm. This is one of the fantastic benefits of fasting—it unclutters our mind so we can taste the fruit of peace. As we feast on peace, we understand that this is what we've been craving all along.

Father, thank you for inviting me to a lifestyle of peace. Thank you for reminding me that regardless of what I'm facing, my soul can be at rest. My mind can know the wonder of quiet contentment. *You* are the peace that surpasses understanding, and if I stay close to you, I will experience all that you offer. My awareness of your presence makes all the difference.

Jesus, you slept through the storm as an example of what I can do by your grace. All I need to do is trust in your love and to remember what you created me to be—courageous, confident, and completely dependent upon your power. If I surrender my worries to your care and recline in your strong arms, you will quell the raging storms within me.

You took my stress, anxiety, and fears to the cross so I could be free. I will not reject the peace you offer just because it contradicts my reasoning. I lay my worries at your feet as a symbol of my commitment to trust you. So come and bring my spirit, soul, and body into alignment with your truth. I choose to believe that peace is your gift to me.

Steps for Transformation

- We decide if we want to walk the path of peace. God will not force us. We've been talking about laying down burdens, trusting God, and listening to his instructions. Consider some other practical things we can do to facilitate an environment of peace in our lives.

- Take a walk through nature, enjoying the sounds, fragrances, and sights. God, in his creative genius, has given these things for you to enjoy. It's calming to be outside, to remember that God, so carefully attentive to the details of creation, cares about every aspect of your life.

- If someone is discussing a subject that creates anxiety, humbly explain that you're staying away from stressful conversations. Then offer another conversation idea. Or, if possible, remove yourself from the conversation altogether.

- Keep worship music playing.

- Take a break from the news.

- Hand over responsibilities, if possible. Be honest with friends, family, or coworkers if you need a break. When our three daughters were young, my husband would give me an hour to myself in the evenings to get quiet before the Lord and recharge.

- Ask the Lord if you're too busy. If he says you are, then be prepared to lay something down.

> *I will not reject the peace you offer just because it contradicts my reasoning. I lay my worries at your feet.*

Scripture to Ponder

Everything I've taught you is so that the peace which is in me will be in you and will give you great confidence as you rest in me.

JOHN 16:33

Suddenly a violent storm developed, with waves so high the boat was about to be swamped. Yet Jesus continued to sleep soundly.

MATTHEW 8:24

Even when your path takes me through
the valley of deepest darkness,
fear will never conquer me, for you already have!
Your authority is my strength and my peace.
The comfort of your love takes away my fear.
I'll never be lonely, for you are near.

PSALM 23:4

DAY 11

Joy

It is time for you to laugh at the enemy's plans, just as the Father does. God created you with joy and for joy. He wants to restore your passion for life, and it may be one reason why he's called you to this fast. Every morning when a new day dawns, anticipate the best instead of dreading the worst—even if all you've experienced lately has been difficult. The fruit of joy grows from a stem that is rooted in God and not the situation. Joy isn't contingent on what's happening to you; it is founded by what's happening within you—in the depths of your spirit where he dwells.

Too often, we hold so tightly to everything wrong that we miss some of God's most glorious blessings. It's time we give ourselves permission to rejoice, dance, and celebrate even when all hell is screaming in our face. No, *especially* when it is. So, let's tap into joy today. Joy that displaces sorrow. Joy that triumphs over tragedy. Joy that confounds the mind but feels absolutely reasonable to our spirits.

Father, I'm tired of trials dictating the way I feel. No longer will I allow emotions, feelings, and circumstances to rule me. Instead, I choose to be joyful. I will let the well of your presence bubble within me and overflow into my thoughts, actions, and reactions. I will enjoy the freedom of laughter and not feel guilty about it. I give you control of my situations and choose to be okay with not being in control of the outcome.

In the presence of my enemy, you have prepared a feast for me. Together at your table, we will laugh at his plans, knowing that nothing on earth can separate me from your love. I can laugh because I trust you. I can stop rehearsing what's wrong because you know how to turn this around for my good. It's okay to lean into joy when things aren't going the way I want. It's okay because I know you're with me, and you're turning my deepest pain into my most significant victory. Instead of wallowing in the mud, I'm going to splash in the puddles. Faith and joy will be my weapons of warfare. I'm brushing off the dry, dusty remains of heaviness and agreeing with joy today. I won't wait another moment.

Steps for Transformation

- One day I was overwhelmed by a situation and couldn't find peace. Tapping into God's presence was impossible because I couldn't stop thinking. I was gripping tightly to the problem and struggling to lay it down. Finally, after a couple of hours of trying to get quiet and hear God, I repented for being stuck in my head. Immediately, the Lord said, *Give yourself permission to stop thinking.* As soon as he said that, I understood that I felt responsible for fixing the problem. I had taken the burden of finding a solution and wouldn't relax until I found one. So, I said, *I give myself one hour to not think about this.* I cranked up the worship music, and God's presence immediately enveloped me. Before long, I was laughing, dancing, and praising God. There was a complete shift. When the hour was up, I didn't pick the problem up again. I knew exactly how the Lord wanted me to handle it. I had so much joy; it was hard to believe how stressed I'd been.

- This is a strategy you can implement. God is giving you permission to experience childlike faith. It isn't irresponsible to stop obsessing. Laughing and trusting God is a key to breakthrough.

> *I have permission to rejoice, dance, and celebrate
> even when all hell is screaming in my face.*

Scripture to Ponder

God-Enthroned merely laughs at them;
the Sovereign One mocks their madness!

PSALM 2:4

I've learned that his anger lasts for a moment,
but his loving favor lasts a lifetime!
We may weep through the night,
but at daybreak it will turn into shouts of ecstatic joy.

PSALM 30:5

Let my passion for life be restored,
tasting joy in every breakthrough you bring to me.
Hold me close to you with a willing spirit
that obeys whatever you say.

PSALM 51:12

DAY 12

Motives

Let's talk about the motives behind our fast. Often during a fast, the Lord strains the debris from our spiritual well so we can take a good hard look at the worldly distractions and anxieties preventing its flow. To embrace freedom, we first have to know what we need to be free from. This fast can be a life-changing event if we invite the Holy Spirit to examine our motives.

If we're fasting to gain the approval of God or a pat on the back from a leader, we're doing it for the wrong reason. We don't fast because we believe it's the only way to get God's attention, shake off shame, or defeat the devil. We refrain from food and deny ourselves because Jesus did it and told us to do it too. However, this isn't about religious obligation. We push the plate away because we're hungry for something food cannot give. We fast because we're already loved and called to a relationship with the Lord that's more intimate and powerful than what we currently have. We believe that we're continually growing from one level of glory to the next and that fasting is a way of fine-tuning ourselves to his Spirit. We fast because we're discovering who we are and who we're called to be.

Lord, I invite you to examine my motives. I don't want to fast out of a fear of rejection, a sense of unworthiness, or because I'm trying to win your approval and earn points. No matter what I do, I can't make myself worthy. Nothing but the price you paid on the cross could ever merit being near you. I'm not afraid that if I don't fast, you'll reject me. I know you love me and will never leave me. Even when I'm not faithful, you are. Regardless of my shortcomings, you love and accept me.

I'm fasting because I love you. I want to refocus my distracted mind and set it fully on you. I submit every thought, word, and deed to your cleansing fire. I dedicate myself to you afresh because nothing matters more than becoming yours unreservedly. Meet with me in my dreams and while I'm awake. Draw me continually, by your grace, to the awareness of your ever-present love. I crave the nearness of your presence and encounters with your glory that impact my life forever.

Steps for Transformation

- Take time to reflect on the question, *Why am I fasting?* People fast for various reasons, and it's essential to find your "why." Be honest with yourself and press in to discover your motivation. Once you've found it, sit with the Lord and share your answer with him.

- Now that you've truthfully expressed your "why," let's go a step further. Quiet the busyness of thoughts and distraction and ask the Lord what *his* "why" is for you. Why has he called you to fast? What is his desire for you during this time? Listen as he speaks to your heart. You may have a gentle idea stirring inside, see a picture in your mind, hear a verse, or discover his answer another way.

- Journal. Write what your motivation for fasting was and how the Lord either confirmed what was on your heart or corrected you. Knowing his purpose will assist in anchoring you when cravings hit or you're tempted to quit. It's a good idea to journal each day of the fast. As the days progress, refer to today's entry to remind yourself why you're doing this.

> *I'm fasting because I love you.*
> *I want to refocus my distracted mind*
> *and set it fully on you.*

Scripture to Ponder

We may think we're right all the time,
but God thoroughly examines our motives.

PROVERBS 21:2

Put your heart and soul into every activity you do,
as though you are doing it for the Lord himself
and not merely for others.

COLOSSIANS 3:23

They all prayed, "Lord Yahweh,
you know the heart of every man."

ACTS 1:24

DAY 13

Yield to the Silence

When we fast, we expect to encounter God. We're all in, diving into times of worship with unrestrained devotion. We've committed to this fast and have set aside time to be with him—to be still and listen, to read and rest. We're excited about what he'll say, the verses that will come alive, or the wisdom he'll impart. Then, to our surprise, everything falls silent.

Sound familiar? Perhaps that's what's happening to you, and you're wondering if you should quit the fast. Don't. One of the most overlooked blessings of fasting is this time of silence. I remember feeling frustrated during a time of seeking the Lord's direction. I didn't hear anything until finally, he spoke to my heart. *If all you hear is silence, yield to it. You will find me there.* I knew he simply wanted me to stay here in the quiet of his presence. After about a week of not hearing, seeing, or understanding what he was doing, only resting in his love, I heard him again. *This is what you needed—just to be with me. You didn't need direction; you needed peace. You needed your mind to be still so I could prepare you for the next step in your life. Now that you are at peace, I can take the lead.*

Today's Prayer

Father, thank you for the silence. For these moments of absolute stillness when you hold me in your arms and soothe my soul with peace. I won't resist them anymore. I will lean back and trust that you know exactly what I need. Give me the grace to resist frustration when I don't hear you. Help me to remember that silence is a blessing and that you're teaching me how to walk the path of peace. Bless me with the ability to wait in your presence, enjoying the honor and beauty of being with my heavenly Father.

You haven't forgotten me. You're not quiet because I've done something wrong. I'm not spiritually dull of hearing; you are just fine-tuning me and sensitizing me to your voice that doesn't always come as I expect. Though sometimes it feels as if you've pulled away, you're actually wooing me closer—into this place of absolute peace and joyful wonder. This is where stress melts away. As I grow comfortable in the quiet, I will hear your whispers of love, and you will heal my soul. I won't resist the silence because I know I will find you in it.

Steps for Transformation

- When we're pressing in for answers, it can feel frustrating to be greeted by silence. But the Lord wants us to be blessed by it. In the quiet, we learn to rest in him, to enjoy the depths of love that are beyond words, to trust and resign ourselves to his timing. Contemplation, which we discussed on day eight, is something we can enjoy every day. Beholding the Lord and choosing to remain quiet before him brings transformation that changes us at our very core.

- If you haven't practiced contemplation, I encourage you to enter into it today. Take note of how you feel. Once you get past the distractions, very often, you will experience a deep sense of peace. Silence has a way of revealing what's inside of you, so if you feel other emotions, don't run from what gets exposed. But be careful not to focus on it either. Simply remain quiet and gently focused on the Lord. All he's looking for is the agreement of your heart so he can do a work that only he can do.

> *If all you hear is silence, yield to it. You will find me there.*

Scripture to Ponder

You're my place of quiet retreat, and your wraparound presence
becomes my shield as I wrap myself in your Word!

PSALM 119:114

He offers a resting place for me in his luxurious love.
His tracks take me to an oasis of peace near *the quiet brook of bliss.*
That's where he restores and revives my life.
He opens before me the right path
and leads me along in his footsteps of righteousness
so that I can bring honor to his name.

PSALM 23:2–3

His left hand cradles my head
while his right hand holds me close.
I am at rest in this love.

SONG OF SONGS 2:6

DAY 14

Trust

Waiting is like a refining fire, burning away superficial religious words like, "I'm *just* trusting God." When all of the forced, counterfeit faith turns to ashes, what remains is the core of our trust—the root of what we believe. Though waiting is painful, it's a blessing in disguise. It reveals where we are, or are not, trusting God. And when we're honest about what we really believe, the Lord blows away the soot, and together we work with him to build a strong foundation.

Trusting God isn't a go-to phrase or last-ditch effort *after* we've done our best to manipulate and control the situation. Faith should be our starting point. If we're doubting and not absolutely convinced that God is in control, then we need to be honest with ourselves and him. From there, we invite the Lord to get to the root of why we are struggling with faith. Knowing the right thing to say doesn't mean our words are coming from a place of absolute honesty and vulnerability. Because fasting helps to expose these areas, we can and should take this time to ask the Holy Spirit to heal any soul wounds that have inhibited our freedom to walk in radical faith.

Today's Prayer

Father, I'm throwing caution to the wind and choosing to trust you. I'm done playing it safe and trying to protect myself from the pain of disappointment. Even if things don't turn out the way I've been praying they would, I believe you love me, are for me, and that you will be with me every step of the way. You are worthy of my unrestrained trust.

Come and heal the wounds of the past that have caused me to doubt. Forgive me for being impatient and taking circumstances into my own hands, as if I can do more than you can. From now on, I will seek your direction and act only under the guidance of your Spirit. Teach me to discern between *my* restless, forced ideas and the God-breathed ones. Awaken the sleeping giant of faith within me. Crush those puny mountains of unbelief that have stood in my way. I don't need to understand all of your ways; I simply need to believe that you love me and that you are good. Lord, encounter me with the reality of your love in a fresh new way. May love become the unshakable foundation of my faith.

Steps for Transformation

- As you read today's devotion, did you sense the Holy Spirit pinpointing something specific? Are there areas where you're struggling to trust him? It's vital to be honest with the Lord and with yourself. The inability to trust is rooted in fear. Fear takes over when we have not fully embraced the love of God. The good news is that God wants to make his love real to you. Let's pray together now and invite him to do just that.

- Father, forgive me for not trusting you. I want nothing to do with unbelief. Make yourself real to me in a new way. Teach me about your love. Pour it out and let it free me from the grip of fear. Heal every area in my soul where I've unwittingly allowed the enemy to torment me with fear and doubt. Give me a revelation of the cross—the price of love that cost you everything so we could be together forever. I lay every concern at your feet and take my hands off, once and for all. I'm ready to trust your love and to give myself to you entirely.

> *Come and heal the wounds of the past*
> *that have caused me to doubt.*
> *May love become the unshakable*
> *foundation of my faith.*

Scripture to Ponder

Your new life began when the Holy Spirit gave you a new birth.
Why then would you so foolishly turn from living in the Spirit
by trying to finish by your own works?

GALATIANS 3:3

Not one promise from God is empty of power.
Nothing is impossible with God!

LUKE 1:37

What does all this mean? If God has determined to stand with
us, tell me, who then could ever stand against us? For God has
proved his love by giving us his greatest treasure, the gift of his Son.
And since God freely offered him up as the sacrifice for us all, he
certainly won't withhold from us anything else he has to give.

ROMANS 8:31–32

DAY 15

Precious Moments

Setting time aside to be in God's presence each day is an essential component of fasting. We mustn't force ourselves to abstain from eating, sticking it out but forgetting that fasting is meant to be a joy. Many have grown accustomed to a time of prayer that equates to nothing more than an all-request hour, instead of precious moments enjoying the beauty of this sacred relationship. Too often, we spend time with the Lord venting and baring our soul but seldom pausing just to adore him. Or, we scour Scripture, not because we're digging for treasure, but because we're trying to impress those who told us that reading the Bible is the right thing to do.

This brilliant, omnipotent, perfect God has chosen to be with us. Let's not overlook the mystery of this! Let's revel in the wonder of it all—our gracious Creator has become our closest friend. He alone deserves our deepest devotion and most heartfelt worship. When we come into a fast, believing for a shift in specific areas of our lives, God woos us into his presence to find it. What he longs to do in our time alone with him is usually much more significant and life-changing than we imagine.

Today's Prayer

Father, I feel you drawing me closer, and I will come. I don't want to pray and fast or read your Word out of duty. I only want to close my eyes, turn my heart to you, and feel the warmth of your embrace. And when your glory overcomes me, I will pour out my tears of unutterable love for you to store in your bottle. So deep is my love for you that words fail me, again and again.

Let my worship please you. Let this fast break the chains that have held me back from walking with you more closely. Help me understand who I am in you so I'm not starving for applause. Purify every desire of my soul so each thought leads to you. May all illusions of grandeur that seek to pull me away from you fade into shadows. This is what I need and nothing more—just to be with you, to discover the joys of uninhibited communion with my Savior and friend. I need to see what natural eyes cannot perceive and to walk in depths of love few others have known. Nothing satisfies me more than encountering the wonder of your presence.

Steps for Transformation

- Are you stuck in a rut? If your time with the Lord has felt boring or forced, God wants to usher you into something new and alive. He wants you to enjoy your relationship. The One who taught the stars to dance and birds to sing is far from dull. Today, spend time with God in a different way from your usual.

- If you normally pray indoors, go outside. A conversation with God can be had in the quiet of your heart anywhere.

- Plan a mini vacation with Jesus. One full day and night alone with him can change your outlook.

- Dress up like you're going out with one of your closest friends and go on a date with the Lord.

- If you normally spend time quietly with the Lord, do the opposite. Crank up the music (put headphones on if necessary) and dance around.

- Find funny videos to watch with him. Jesus is full of joy and wants you to be too.

- Write him a letter and tell him all of the things you love about him, then ask him what he loves about you and write them down.

- Remember, he's not only your Lord; he wants to be your best friend.

> *So deep is my love for you*
> *that words fail me,*
> *again and again.*

Scripture to Ponder

Move your heart closer and closer to God,
and he will come even closer to you.
But make sure you cleanse your life, you sinners,
and keep your heart pure and stop doubting.

JAMES 4:8

Because of you, I know the path of life,
as I taste the fullness of joy in your presence.
At your right side I experience divine pleasures forevermore!

PSALM 16:11

We have come into an intimate experience with God's love, and we
trust in the love he has for us. God is love! Those who are living in
love are living in God, and God lives through them.

1 JOHN 4:16

DAY 16

The Mind of Christ

Our mind has dominated our feelings and decisions for too long. As triune beings made up of spirit, soul, and body, we come into proper alignment when we let our spirit lead instead of our mind. Our spirit, in submission to God's Spirit, walks in agreement with God. This is why our minds must not be allowed to rule our lives.

It seems we've become accustomed to thoughts taking a position of authority. We lazily sit back and ignore the multitude of unhealthy, untrue, and damaging ideas that run through our heads, as if they have the right to torment us. On the flip side, we mustn't obsess over every thought. The answer is to submit each one to the Lord and to make his presence a sanctuary for mental health. And to make a habit of pausing and acknowledging him throughout the day, especially in times of busyness and stress. This should be more than a quick mental greeting that doesn't touch our hearts. When we purposefully take time to stop, close our eyes, and calmly become aware of his love, we are strengthening our spirits and forcing our minds to yield to his lordship. This is something we can do whether or not we're fasting, but fasting helps tune us in to him more readily.

Father, I want to recognize the reality of your nearness continually. Even now, I feel you drawing me into your presence and letting me know that I can remain aware of you at all times. Remind me often to bring every thought into the cleansing flow of your glory. Help me to notice when things I'm meditating on are not in agreement with your truth. Make it obvious when the images in my head are founded on nothing more than lies, fears, unhealthy habits, or a need to control what feels out of control.

Jesus, be the Lord of every unconscious musing, the center of all I think and feel. May every thought bow to your majesty. When the enemy bombards me with distractions and seeks to lead me astray, stir your Word within me so truth rises to the surface. When doubts and questions claw at my mind, remind me to lay them at your feet as an offering of trust. Lord, hold my mind in the grace that comes by remaining in your presence. As I intentionally set my mind on you, wrap my imagination with a covering of peace, and let my thoughts align with what my spirit knows to be true. Silence the screaming chaos with the whispers of your love.

Steps for Transformation

- If a continual awareness of God is your desire, it is a desire given to you by him. Though it sometimes seems a difficult task to guard the heart and mind in such a way that the Lord is your constant awareness, it isn't. He wouldn't have told you to set your mind on things above if you weren't able to do it with his help (see Colossians 3:2). He is the One who stirred this longing in you, and he promises to give you the desires of your heart that are in alignment with his. All he is looking for is your agreement.

- When your thoughts drift from him, don't feel guilty. Instead, gently turn your attention back to him. Because he lives inside of you, reconnecting with his presence is as easy as a change of focus.

- Don't ignore the soft wooing of his Spirit throughout the day. Listen as he whispers to you even in times of busyness. If you'll make his presence your delight and choose to engage with him, instead of putting it off until later, you may be surprised by the shift in your peace and joy.

> *Silence the screaming chaos*
> *with the whispers of your love.*

Scripture to Ponder

Feast on all the treasures of the heavenly realm and fill your
thoughts with heavenly realities, and not with the distractions
of the natural realm.

COLOSSIANS 3:2

Who has ever intimately known the mind of the Lord Yahweh
well enough to become his counselor? Christ has, and we possess
Christ's perceptions.

1 CORINTHIANS 2:16

We can demolish every deceptive fantasy that opposes God and
break through every arrogant attitude that is raised up in defiance of
the true knowledge of God. We capture, like prisoners of war, every
thought and insist that it bow in obedience to the Anointed One.

2 CORINTHIANS 10:5

DAY 17

The Power of Humility

Fasting is a way of humbling ourselves. It invites us to remember the magnificence of mercy and causes us to bow low in gratefulness. It sets us upon a sure foundation of grace—nothing we have done or ever can do has earned our place of favor with the Lord. It is a beautiful gift. We don't become prideful in our identity, as if we had anything to do with it. Apart from him, we are nothing. We don't boast about our religious duties but delight in truth—it's only because of love that we stand.

Humility is an empowering posture, and by taking this stance, we declare the lordship of Jesus. We echo his absolute dependence upon the Father. Understanding who we are should provoke a humble posture of gratitude, never inflame an attitude of entitlement. To think that he has entrusted his glory to frail earthen vessels is mindboggling. We were birthed by the wounds of Christ, and the evidence of his glory rises to the surface of our lives when we choose to go low. Here, he reveals himself to us and subdues our fleshly, defiant, and sinful natures. Only a humble heart receives correction with gratefulness and then, through unconditional surrender, rises in power.

Father, I'm aware of my great need for you. In my desire to honor you, help me not to focus on doing everything right but to walk in sincerity of heart. I aim to please you alone, not by working to earn your approval but by remaining dependent upon your grace. If a need for fleshly recognition has tainted my motives for fasting, reveal my sin. I long to live without hindrances to the sweetness of our relationship.

Lord, as I become more confident in my position in you, help me to remain humble and to remember daily that it is only by grace that I stand. It is only because of the gifts you've given me that I have something to offer. Though I courageously do what you've placed in my heart, I will walk hand in hand with you, completely reliant upon your strength. May I never run ahead in pride or lag behind in fear. May I not only love and honor your Spirit in me but treat others with respect and love as well. I am a habitation of your glory, but it is only by bowing low that your glory pours out. I can do all things *only* when I do them with you.

Steps for Transformation

- The moment we think we're humble is the moment we reveal that we aren't. Walking in humility isn't a forced action. It is a posture of dependence that keeps its eyes on Jesus so he can lead by example. Once we acknowledge the pride in our lives and ask God to forgive us, the only thing left to do is to behold the Lord in his humility. He will expose prideful motives, actions, and words. He will cleanse our hearts and show us a more excellent way.

- Pride is subtle. It tries to sneak into conversations, looking for recognition and attention. Bragging, name dropping, refusing to apologize, criticizing, always talking about ourselves—these are just some of the ways pride manifests. But instead of focusing on what we're doing wrong, let's rejoice in God's mercy and grace. How blessed we are to see the sins that keep us from walking in purity. It is by his grace that we stand.

- Let's pray: *Father, I want nothing to do with pride. Cleanse me, purify my heart, and teach me how to emulate Jesus in his humility. I want to bring you glory in every area of my life.*

> *I am a habitation of your glory, but it is only by bowing low that your glory pours out. I can do all things only when I do them with you.*

Scripture to Ponder

I'm trained in the secret of overcoming all things, whether in fullness or in hunger. And I find that the strength of Christ's explosive power infuses me to conquer every difficulty.

PHILIPPIANS 4:12–13

I'm obviously not trying to flatter you or water down my message to be popular with men, but my supreme passion is to please God. For if all I attempt to do is please people, I would fail to be a true servant of Christ.

GALATIANS 1:10

Have you forgotten that your body is now the sacred temple of the Spirit of Holiness, who lives in you? You don't belong to yourself any longer, for the gift of God, the Holy Spirit, lives inside your sanctuary.

1 CORINTHIANS 6:19

DAY 18

Merciful Love

God's love is relentless and alive. It roars with a passion that arrests our hearts and reminds us of who we are. It whispers with such depth that our entire beings reverberate with life. Every imperfection has been defeated in the victory of his merciful compassion. Nothing could stop the Lord from demolishing every obstacle that separated us from him. We are the ones he longed for.

Before we knew what was happening, love awakened us and revived our hearts. Love brought us near but yearns for us to be nearer still, to cast aside our restrictions and run without reservations into his loving arms. Jesus is always pursuing us. He gazes at us continually and never looks away. He is the perfect example of untainted, unselfish love. Let's allow this time of fasting to draw us into the bliss of unspeakable encounters with Jesus, who paid everything to be with us. As we entirely resign ourselves to the One whose holy love is fierce and unstoppable, gentle, and compassionate, everything about us changes. We want nothing more than to be consumed with his glory. And this glory, this palpable presence, is what makes fasting enjoyable, satisfying, and life-changing. We are his beloved, and his merciful love has set us free.

Today's Prayer

Jesus, hold me in your arms forever. I'm lovesick and am unwilling to live with falsity or be bullied into religious duties. Nothing matters more than being yours, unreservedly. I want every part of me, spirit, soul, and body, to sense the abundance of your love. My lifetime pursuit is to know you more than anyone has ever known you before, to be content in the wonder of this love, and to be with you forever.

On days when I allow the cares of life to distract me from you, draw me by your Spirit into the quiet of your arms. Mercifully wrap me in the stillness of your presence until every fiber of my being is saturated with your ever-present love. Your patience astounds me. Your grace sustains me. May I never doubt, never strain to enter into your presence when it's so readily available. Lord, come with waves of unrestrained glory and crash upon my soul until love is the only standing foundation. All I need to do is breathe deep and sink into the ocean of your affection. May I rapture your heart as you have raptured mine.

Steps for Transformation

- Nothing changes us more than the love of God. We can live in this place of holy encounter every day, where love continually transforms us in the very depths of our hearts. But sometimes we get sidetracked by busyness and stress. Perhaps shaking off anxiety is part of why you started this fast. Regaining this place of intimacy is a holy desire that God will not ignore.

- Write a love letter to Jesus. You don't have to be a writer to open your heart and express it. The point of this exercise isn't to wax eloquent (unless you want to). The purpose is to help you refocus, to remember why you love him, and to convey your love and commitment. Who is he to you? What has he done to bless you and prove his love? Tell him what you see when you behold him. What stirs when you look into his eyes? How do you want to live? What are you grateful for? What do you love about him? Pour out your heart without restraint or a need to make the letter perfect.

> *Lord, come with waves of unrestrained glory and crash upon my soul until love is the only standing foundation.*

Scripture to Ponder

Revive me with your raisin cakes.
Refresh me again with your apples.
Help me and hold me, for I am lovesick!
I am longing for more—
yet how could I take more?

SONG OF SONGS 2:5

Arise, my dearest. Hurry, my darling.
Come away with me!
I have come as you have asked
to draw you to my heart and lead you out.
For now is the time, my beautiful one.

SONG OF SONGS 2:10

O my beloved, you are lovely.
When I see you in your beauty,
I see a radiant city where we will dwell as one.
More pleasing than any pleasure,
more delightful than any delight,
you have ravished my heart,
stealing away my strength to resist you.

SONG OF SONGS 6:4

DAY 19

Fear Must Go

Fear contradicts the will of God for your life. You were not created to continually worry, letting worse case scenarios play out in your head. It's time to be free from fear and to stop giving it a place of authority in your life. This is your season to break the habit of negative expectations by choosing to align with God's truth.

Fasting is an excellent bondage breaker. It is an incredible tool for subduing the fleshly nature. God doesn't stand at a distance, pointing out what's wrong. Instead, he draws close, infusing himself into every shadow. Light always drives out darkness. Faith pushes fear far from your soul and empowers you with confidence.

Love is the foundation for trusting God. Love anchors you to peace. There is no other way around it. Grounding yourself in God's love is what makes the difference. Fear doesn't play fair. It lurks around every corner waiting for an opportunity to drag you back into its foggy arena. When that happens, kick it out. Just because you initially feel fear doesn't mean you have to allow it to continually take up space in your heart. Become accustomed to walking in the love of God and committed to staying in peace. The choice is yours.

Father, fear will not rule me any longer. I repent for behaving as though I'm not strong enough to defeat it when the same Spirit that raised Jesus from the grave lives inside of me! It's time for me to agree with your truth, to become so acquainted with your perfect love that I laugh at fear when it dares to come close, to dive so deeply into your love that fear's voice is barely discernable. This is where I want to live—in the protection of your love.

Indeed, things haven't always gone the way I wanted. But I will no longer allow fear to sit as master upon the throne that was designed for you. My heart cries, *Come and be my Lord!* Free me from the grip of negative expectations. From this point on, write my story with a pen of redemption. It's time for me to believe for the outrageous and extraordinary so faith becomes the legacy I leave behind. I believe because I've chosen to unite all that I am with you. I overcome fear simply because I am submerged in your love.

Steps for Transformation

- God wants us to be free from fear. Jesus repeatedly told us in Scripture not to fear, so it must be possible to overcome. Fear grows when we give tormenting thoughts attention. It loses its hold when we find God's truth on the matter.

- If you've been dealing with fear, I strongly suggest soaking in God's love. Put some worship music on and tune out everything else until you feel his presence. Once your mind is at rest and peaceful, bring each fear to the Lord and lay them at his feet.

- Replace each lie with his truth. Search his Word for passages that minister hope and life. Then meditate on them until they get past your mind and into your heart. Let the combination of his love and his Word be like oil to your soul, causing fear to slide off easily.

- Fear often pushes us to take control. Only act when God tells you to. If there's something he wants you to do, you'll need to stay at peace to hear his instructions.

- Remember, just because the enemy throws a fearful thought at you doesn't mean you have to agree with it. As soon as you notice it, command it to go in Jesus' name. Then fix your gaze on the Lord.

> *I will no longer allow fear to sit as master*
> *upon the throne that was designed for you.*

Scripture to Ponder

Love never brings fear, for fear is always related to punishment. But love's perfection drives the fear of punishment far from our hearts. Whoever walks constantly afraid of punishment has not reached love's perfection.

1 JOHN 4:18

This is the kind of fast that I desire:
Remove the heavy chains of oppression!
Stop exploiting your workers!
Set free the crushed and mistreated!
Break off every yoke of bondage!
Share your food with the hungry!
Provide for the homeless and bring them into your home!
Clothe the naked!
Don't turn your back on your own flesh and blood!
Then my favor will bathe you in sunlight
until you are like the dawn bursting through a dark night.
And then suddenly your healing will manifest.
You will see your righteousness march out before you,
and the glory of Yahweh will protect you from all harm!
Then Yahweh will answer you when you pray.
When you cry out for help, he will say,
"I am here."

ISAIAH 58:6–9

DAY 20

Adoration

What if we spent time with the Lord, not only to receive but to give? Prayer is about connection and relationship with the One who taught our hearts to beat and whose voice stirs the wind. Yes, Jesus wants us to ask for the things we need. Yes, he wants us to freely share the burdens and desires of our hearts with him. But how much of our prayer time is spent lavishing the Lord with words of adoration and praise? How often do we bring him an offering of unselfish love, seeking nothing in return? Are we making prayer and fasting about our desires or about discovering his?

What if we bowed before him and did nothing besides pouring out our hearts of devotion and thanksgiving? Today, let's set time aside to tell the Lord how absolutely lovesick and grateful we are. Let's be intentional about getting ourselves off our minds and make it our aim to shower him with honor and praise. It is our privilege to lay aside our needs and captivate him with our love. He deserves so much more than we could ever give. Let's come into his presence, simply to bless the One who ceaselessly blesses us.

Father, I don't tell you enough how much I love you. I am overflowing with gratitude—undone by your faithfulness. You have been so good to me, and all I want to do is show my adoration for you with my unrestrained praise. I will not restrict my tears or hold back my cries of love. You have welcomed me into your chambers, so I come with gifts of untethered praise and complete sincerity. My greatest desire is to honor you with my life—my total and complete devotion.

I want my love to arrest your attention, each word of affection to be sincere, and every syllable to rise to you like a sweet perfume. I bless you with my worship. With my life. With my absolute surrender. I'm holding nothing back. You deserve my song, my dance, and every shout of praise. Even if I spent every ounce of strength to demonstrate my love, it wouldn't be enough. You, my first love, deserve more than I could possibly give. Though my words are often few and my love weak, my desire is sincere. My surrender is complete. I am yours forever.

Steps for Transformation

- When God's tangible love envelops us, it is nothing short of incredible. Nothing shifts our attention away from stress like one encounter with his presence. But what if we came to him for no other reason than to pour out our love? Honoring the Lord with adoration that seeks nothing other than to bless him is a blessing that has no comparison. What a joy it is to know that the Creator of all, the Ancient of Days who is holy and perfect, desires our worship. The thought is incomprehensible yet true.

- I encourage you to spend today lavishing the Lord with words of love that overflow from your heart. Ask him for nothing. Let today be an offering unto him. A day to praise him and remember his goodness, faithfulness, majesty, and power. A day to seek nothing for yourself. And if contrary thoughts or any self-seeking rise up, tell them to take their place before the King. Commit every part of this day to bless the One who is continually blessing you.

> *Let every syllable rise to you
> like sweet perfume.*

Scripture to Ponder

As the king surrounded me at his table,
the sweet fragrance of spikenard awakened the night.

SONG OF SONGS 1:12

I know that you will welcome me into your house,
for I am covered by your covenant of mercy and love.
So I come to your sanctuary with deepest awe
to bow in worship and adore you.

PSALM 5:7

This is what the Lord says about these people:
"They come near to me with hollow words
and honor me superficially with their lips;
all the while their hearts run far away from me!
Their worship is nothing more than man-made rules."

ISAIAH 29:13

DAY 21

Processing Emotions

Emotions are gifts from God. They allow us to tune in to what's happening inside. They create space for deeper thoughts, creativity, and union with God. They invite us into the divine by helping us step out of the limiting factors of analytical thinking. But they can also drag us down if we don't process them with the Lord and invite his refining fire to burn at the center of all we feel.

Fasting helps us step back from the swirls of mental overload and gracefully sink into a space we've carved out for the Lord. A place where light exposes hidden lies and unhealthy beliefs. A promised "safe-place" where we view our life from God's perspective. As we resign ourselves to his wisdom, he speaks the truth that drowns every lie. We discover that emotions are meant to serve us, not rule over us. When we're aware of our feelings and bring them before his glory, he reveals our real, most vulnerable beliefs—the areas we haven't fully surrendered.

Today, invite the Lord into the strongest negative emotion you've been experiencing and ask for his perspective.

Today's Prayer

Father, forgive me for allowing negative emotions to master my minutes, days, or years. Help me to align my thoughts and beliefs with your truth so every emotion leads to you, instead of dragging me away. I don't want to live from my soul; I want to live from my spirit—from the reality of *your* Spirit in me. From the abundant joy of living face-to-face with my Father, Lord, friend, and King. I long to be stable, unmovable in my faith, and to experience joy and peace that contradict every trial.

Unravel the unhealthy beliefs that have intricately woven themselves into my identity. Teach me who I am in you so perfect love births tenacious trust. Forgive me for focusing on negative feelings instead of bringing them immediately to you. Expose the lies I've believed—the subtle tricks of the enemy that have disconnected me from your gift of freedom. Enable me to discern what fuels every emotion so I won't be drawn into deception. Help me to be honest about what I feel so every thought directs me to the One whose glory sets me free.

Steps for Transformation

- What have you been thinking about? If you're not sure, listen to what's been coming out of your mouth. The subject of your conversations will reveal the occupation of your heart. If your mind has been swirling in a multitude of directions, sit down and write out each concern. It's important to know what is weighing on you. When it comes to negative emotions, fear is often at the root. Sometimes the fear of something is more tormenting than the thing we fear. Face fears with the Lord by confessing them and asking for his perspective.

- Faith is the antidote for fear. And faith comes by hearing what God has to say. God has set a feast before us in the form of Scripture. Ask the Holy Spirit to give you verses that reflect his truth for you in this season. Study them. Write them out. Meditate on them, slowly. Invite the Lord to tell you exactly what he's teaching you. Refer back to these verses throughout the day and week and declare them. It's not enough to habitually confess his Word; we must believe. Truly believe. It must become a reality in our hearts.

> *Teach me who I am in you so*
> *perfect love births tenacious trust.*

Scripture to Ponder

Perfect, absolute peace surrounds those
whose imaginations are consumed with you;
they confidently trust in you.

Isaiah 26:3

May the words of my mouth, my meditation-thoughts,
and every movement of my heart be always pure and pleasing,
acceptable before your eyes, Yahweh,
my only Redeemer, my Protector.

Psalm 19:14

To be transformed as you embrace the glorious Christ-within as
your new life and live in union with him! For God has re-created
you all over again in his perfect righteousness, and you now belong
to him in the realm of true holiness.

Ephesians 4:24

DAY 22

Something New

When God calls us to a fast, we usually don't know what he has in store, but our trust in him assures us that it must be good. While we don't always understand his plans, we unite faith with action and follow his lead. Fasts are often birthed by a longing in our hearts for something new, even if we're not sure what that is. We may be experiencing a dissatisfaction that is fueled by a holy desire for greater intimacy with the Lord. Perhaps we feel stagnant or stifled. Or maybe we sense a coming shift in our life, so with focused intention, we turn to the Lord with fasting.

Fasts can be a divine connecting point where God escorts us from one level of glory to the next. As if a secret entrance has opened in response to our yearning hearts. However, to squeeze through this narrow passageway, we bow, relinquishing old mindsets and anything that restricts forward movement. At the entrance, we offer our desire to remain in control of our lives. As we surrender all—every frustration, disappointment, and even our dreams and aspirations—we find a freedom that cannot be defined by human logic. As we yield to him, we always discover something new. As we step into him, we find all that we've ever wanted.

Father, amid my hopes and dreams or feelings of dissatisfaction and frustration, I find one consistency—my continual need for you. You stand at the center of it all, and I have no desire to reach for anything else. You are the epicenter of absolute fulfillment—the foundation of my life. You are the One who restores my sense of balance when things feel wobbly and unsure. You are the balm of peace when my soul feels frazzled.

You have heard my cry to become yours, unconditionally. Unchain my soul from anything that hinders the reality of heaven in my life. I want nothing to rule me except for you. Fine-tune my spirit so nothing distorts your voice or causes dismay. In your wisdom, use seasons of dissatisfaction as a catapult to launch me into the most significant breakthroughs I've ever known. May this fast facilitate a mindset shift that untangles the web of unhealthy thoughts and ignites my faith anew. I offer you all that I am and lay aside everything that has restricted me. I want to be fully present with you at all times, instead of wholly consumed by problems. I'm ready to step into the new things you have for me, Lord.

Steps for Transformation

- When you wake up in the morning, what is the first thing you think about? Is it your prewritten to-do list? Thoughts of yesterday? Images of what's going wrong in your life? You are a powerful person because the same Spirit that raised Jesus from the dead lives inside of you. And as a powerful person, you can choose what you think about when you wake up and when you go to sleep.

- Tonight, before you close your eyes, do a quick run-through of the day's events. Leave every concern in God's hands and fall asleep thinking of him, instead of your problems. This will help keep you open to receive from his Spirit in your sleep. And by focusing on him instead of issues, you're more likely to have sweet sleep.

- When you wake, ask him to help you form a new habit—one of starting your day by immediately turning to him. Each day, ask the Lord what's on his heart. Ask him to lead you. By doing these things every day, his presence becomes habitual. I cannot think of a better way to start and end your day.

> *You stand at the center of it all,
> and I have no desire to reach for
> anything else. You are the epicenter
> of absolute fulfillment.*

Scripture to Ponder

We can all draw close to him with the veil removed from our faces.
And with no veil we all become like mirrors who brightly reflect
the glory of the Lord Jesus. We are being transfigured into his very
image as we move from one brighter level of glory to another. And
this glorious transfiguration comes from the Lord, who is the Spirit.

2 Corinthians 3:18

It is through him that we live and function and have our identity;
just as your own poets have said, "Our lineage comes from him."

Acts 17:28

Blissful are your eyes, for they see.
Delighted are your ears,
for they are open to hear all these things.

Matthew 13:16

Our Most Holy Pursuit

We're all searching for that one thing. Longing for an end to our soul's unrest. Clamoring for peace. Reaching for joy and wondering where and when we lost it. Running after a love that already exists inside of us—waiting for *us* to be still and know. And this is the crux of it all—to *know*. To be entirely convinced that every joy and solace of the soul are found in him.

We can search the whole world for something to fill the void echoing inside of us, and we may find pleasures that satisfy temporarily. But until we come to the end of ourselves and recognize that the Lord not only is our connecting point to fulfillment but also *is* our fulfillment, nothing will change.

The Lord must become our most holy pursuit. The One we live for. Surrender to. He is that *One thing* that sets everything else in order. He is the only One who satisfies every aspect of our life and makes it worth living. He is our joy. Our peace. Jesus is the source of freedom. The One who loves us unconditionally and reminds us that we belong.

Today's Prayer

Lord, come close and let your breath awaken my soul. In my quest to acquire peace and joy, I finally realize that you are the source of all I need. Forgive me for looking outside of you. You are my everything. In you, I am perfectly loved and safely held. I'm not only resilient but also protected—impenetrable by the cares of this world. No longer will I clamor and strive for a temporary fix. I won't be deceived by the pleasures of this world that last for a moment. I long to live in the eternal joys of heaven that are found in you, right now.

As I set my affection on you and allow my mind to step back, my spirit comes alive. My very being is absorbed by the reality of your overwhelming love. You are the One I adore. The One I need more than anyone else. The One who gave all he had just to be with me. Pouring myself out to you is my greatest honor. Living for you has made me come alive. Knowing you love me and always have my best interests at heart causes me to rejoice and allows my soul to rest.

Steps for Transformation

- What do you believe will make you happy? So many are waiting for that one thing (or multiple things) to happen so they can finally be happy. But our greatest victory comes when we find absolute contentment and joy that stands outside of circumstances. Joy that is positioned in him. Today, come back to first-love fulfillment. Ask the Lord to make his presence real again. He wants you to have the desires of your heart, but it is his presence that purifies dreams and keeps them in proper perspective.

- Remember, it is through the Lord that the things we're reaching for are best accessed. When we force our ways and timing, we become frustrated and anxious. But when we set our focus on him and set every dream before him in perfect trust, he paves the way with grace. Ask him to reveal the areas where you're not trusting him. Be honest about desires that have stolen your affections and have become more important than the sweetness of his presence. Every hope and dream matters to the Lord, but he wants you to find contentment in him first. In his presence is fullness of joy.

> *I long to live in the eternal joys of heaven*
> *that are found in you, right now.*

Scripture to Ponder

My soul thirsts, pants, and longs for the living God.
I want to come and see the face of God.

PSALM 42:2

We view our slight, short-lived troubles in the light of eternity. We
see our difficulties as the substance that produces for us an eternal,
weighty glory far beyond all comparison, because we don't focus
our attention on what is seen but on what is unseen. For what is
seen is temporary, but the unseen realm is eternal.

2 CORINTHIANS 4:17–18

In the depths of my heart I truly know
that you, Yahweh, have become my Shield;
You take me and surround me with yourself.
Your glory covers me continually.
You lift high my head.

PSALM 3:3

DAY 24

Hands Off

This posture of humbling ourselves in fasting is one we should never rise from. It is a position of dependency that must frame our lives. One beautiful attribute of the believer is our reliance upon our Father. It is expressed by our attitudes and actions when things are out of our control. If we say we trust him but continuously try to fix everything and everyone, then we're living under a shadow of deception—a heavy darkness named pride.

Humility releases what it doesn't understand. It is a hands-off approach that isn't accompanied by irritation or defiance but is characterized by tenderness and trust in God. Pride pushes us to take matters in our own hands. It drives us to find answers and to make things right without hearing God's directions. Until we unmask the subtle ways of pride that fight to have their way, we won't understand those instructions. We won't know his will when our will is more important to us.

So, during this time of fasting, pay attention to what irritates you, concerns you, and triggers your need to take over. These are the areas where pride may be hindering your most glorious breakthroughs.

Father, open my eyes to see the areas where I'm fighting to maintain control. Point out the situations where I'm not trusting you. I want nothing to do with control or self-power because they are rooted in pride. Instead of holding tightly to my idea of the way things should be, I open my hands and ask you to remove what doesn't belong. I release every desire that does not point to you or that causes me to fight to have my way. Pour out your grace.

You are my heart's desire. My need to remain aware of you at all times has me on my knees. I can do nothing without you. I cannot love purely or live unselfishly without your help. I don't even know how to approach the day unless I first find you in it. Lord, I am totally and utterly dependent upon you. Lead me. As I quiet myself in your presence, speak clearly. I submit my will, my plans, my attitudes, and the need for things to be the way *I* want them to be because I trust you. Let my overwhelming need for you keep me here in the safety of continual surrender. I let go and trust you fully. Take over, Lord.

Steps for Transformation

- In the prayer above, you asked the Lord to reveal areas where you're not trusting him or are still holding tightly to control. I encourage you to write down what he said. Throughout the day, remain aware of thoughts, actions, or words that contradict faith or put you in the driver's seat. Don't ignore anything that the Holy Spirit highlights. When you notice these tendencies to fear, worry, or take control, acknowledge them with a repentant heart, thank God for his grace, and return your gaze to him.

- With your gaze on the Lord, remember that he, too, looked to our Father for guidance. Jesus was dependent upon his Father and demonstrated humility by only doing what he saw the Father doing. Let's follow the Lord's example by acknowledging him in every decision. I think we may be surprised at how we've taken our lives into our hands. But humble trust will free us and open the door for God to show himself strong. By fixing our eyes on the Lord, his Spirit will guide us into all truth (see Psalm 43:3 and John 16:13).

> *Instead of holding tightly to my idea of the way things should be, I open my hands and ask you to remove what doesn't belong.*

Scripture to Ponder

Everyone who knows your wonderful name
keeps putting their trust in you.
They can count on you for help no matter what.
O Lord, you will never, no never, neglect those who come to you.

PSALM 9:10

Nothing I do is from my own initiative. As I hear the judgment passed by my Father, I execute those judgments. And my judgments will be perfect, because I seek only to fulfill the desires of my Father who sent me.

JOHN 5:30

What is the cause of your conflicts and quarrels with each other? Doesn't the battle begin inside of you as you fight to have your own way and fulfill your own desires?

JAMES 4:1

DAY 25

This is Our Honor

Fasting and prayer are an honor. What an incredible privilege we have to stand before our King and call him Father and friend. This is our opportunity to offer ourselves, spirit, soul, and body, to empty ourselves of distractions and seek him above all we want and need. This heart stance is a gift. We cannot take credit for the love we feel toward him, yet we can steward it with tender care and great appreciation.

Fasting doesn't force God's hand, but there is something mysterious about fasting that seems to move his heart, especially when large groups unite in prayer and fasting. We're not doing it to earn his love. He already loves us as much as he ever will. We already have his attention, whether we're fasting or not. Pushing aside the plate and prostrating ourselves before the Lord reminds us of our great need for his guidance, empowerment, wisdom, and grace. We remember that without him, we are nothing. As we humble ourselves, we honor him. When we deny our natural appetite and declare that our longing to know the Lord is more urgent than food, it glorifies him. It isn't about forcing God to act on our behalf. It's about denying a basic human need and declaring that our need for him is more significant.

Father, forgive me if I've inadvertently thought of fasting as a way to force your hand or earn your help. You are my provider, healer, and the One who destroys the yoke of oppression. And although specific requests rise from my heart that only you can meet, I never want to view you as my butler whom I expect to perform my every request. I need *you*. I want *you*. You are the single most important thing in my life. You are the One I love. The One who makes life worth living.

And so, I set my heart on this holy quest—to know you and to be found *in* you because it's in you that I live, function, and find my identity. I choose to be more focused on the beauty of your presence than the joy of your blessing. I want to esteem you the way you deserve, to praise and worship you from a position of absolute devotion and gratefulness. You have done all that was needed for us to be unceasingly connected. You set me up to experience a life of victory by living in union with you. Thank you for allowing me to honor you with this fast. I choose to seek your face, your ways, and your love more than my daily bread.

Steps for Transformation

- Sometimes, especially in long fasts, we lose sight of why we began the fast. Refraining from certain foods or activities may still sting a bit, but after some time, it becomes a habit, and we disconnect from the heart behind it. Because this fast is focused on intimacy with the Lord, it's vital to enjoy quality time with him every day. If possible, try to extend it. Wake earlier, skip television or mindless searching on the web, and use those hours to worship, spend time in contemplation, or meditate on the Word.

- Even if you already spend a great deal of time with him, you may discover that it's not sufficient. One hour may have felt like a lot, but suddenly, two hours aren't enough. Your passion is growing, and now it's essential to fan the flame continually. For many, the Lord is creating new habits that he wants you to continue once the fast is over. Regardless of how much alone time with him you get, ask the Father if he's inviting you to enjoy more.

> *I set my heart on this holy quest—*
> *to know you.*

Scripture to Ponder

I am standing in absolute stillness,
silent before the one I love,
waiting as long as it takes for him to rescue me.
Only God is my Savior, and he will not fail me.

PSALM 62:5

Jesus answered him, "'Love the Lord your God with every passion of
your heart, with all the energy of your being, and with every thought
that is within you.' This is the great and supreme commandment."

MATTHEW 22:37–38

Arise, my love.
Open your heart, my darling, deeper still to me.
Will you receive me this dark night?
There is no one else but you, my friend, my equal.
I need you this night to arise and come be with me.
You are my pure, loyal dove, a perfect partner for me.
My flawless one, will you arise?
For my heaviness and tears are more than I can bear.
I have spent myself for you throughout the dark night.

SONG OF SONGS 5:2

DAY 26

Hearing God

Something many of us hope to gain during a fast is a clear sense of the Lord's direction. We want to hear him and know his will. But often our expectations about *how* he'll speak causes us to miss what he's saying. In desperation, we put pressure on ourselves to hear, anxiously scouring his Word or trying to access with our minds what can only be heard with the heart. Perhaps we don't believe we have his attention—as if turning our hearts to him isn't enough.

Our Father loves communicating with us, and he knows how to speak to the ones he's created. We set ourselves up for disappointment when we expect to hear him in a specific way. The creative avenues he'll use to reveal his will are unlimited. He can guide us through dreams or sovereign encounters that paint clear visuals of his will. Quite often, he speaks in the quiet of our hearts through his Word and rarely in an audible voice. The Lord also directs us through articles, devotionals, emails, a random message from a friend, a movie, or a sign on the side of a road. If we don't limit him and we keep ourselves open and expectant, we'll notice he has been speaking and guiding us more than we've realized.

Father, I open my heart to you, unreservedly. Expectantly. Holy Spirit, help me not to miss your subtle nudges or loud exclamations that come in wonderfully unpredictable ways. I won't strive to hear you; I won't stress as I learn to discern your voice. I will simply believe you know exactly how to get my attention. You are the good and faithful Shepherd who knows how to lead and care for me. All you're looking for is the agreement of my faith.

Even if I don't find the certainty of your desire in the midst of this fast, I know you will reveal everything I need to know in time. You're here. You've heard my prayers, and now I wait, tuning in to you with faith, joy, and peace-filled anticipation. I will practice quieting my soul to tap into the sound of your Spirit rising within me. I will remain spiritually awake, ready, and waiting for you to speak in whatever way you choose. Instead of anxiously hoping to know your will, I will trust and believe that you love to unveil it. Clarity will come, and whether it is revealed instantly, or slowly over weeks, months, or years, I know you never let me down.

Steps for Transformation

- How has the Lord been speaking to you over the past week? Grab your journal and sit quietly in the Lord's presence. Ask him to highlight conversations, random thoughts, images, verses, articles, or other ways he's been communicating with you. Too often, something catches our attention, but we chalk it up to coincidence and ignore it. Or we get excited that he's speaking or confirming but move on quickly and forget. Let's make a habit of pausing as soon as something speaks to us and writing it down. Get used to carrying a small journal or use the Notes app on your phone to jot down what you're receiving from the Lord. You may be surprised how often he's speaking to you.

- If the Lord has been highlighting specific Bible passages, be diligent to pay attention. Write out a few that he's been pointing out and focus on them over the next few days, weeks, or as long as you sense your spirit feasting on them. Ponder them throughout the day and ask the Lord to reveal what he wants you to glean from what he's saying.

> *You've heard my prayers,*
> *and now I wait, tuning in to you*
> *with faith, joy, and peace-filled anticipation.*

Scripture to Ponder

My own sheep will hear my voice
and I know each one,
and they will follow me.

JOHN 10:27

The only way people come to me is by the Father who sent me—
he pulls on their hearts to embrace me. And those who are drawn
to me, I will certainly raise them up in the last day.

JOHN 6:44

Listen! I hear my lover's voice.
I know it's him coming to me—
leaping with joy over mountains,
skipping in love over the hills that separate us,
to come to me.

SONG OF SONGS 2:8

DAY 27

The Well of Grace

The sacrifice of fasting is both powerful and private. It is an expression of surrender that comes from a heart intent on encountering God in every area of our being. It's a decision to step away from the temporary satisfaction of food to embrace the eternal sufficiency of Christ. Let's never underestimate the importance of a heart so intent on discovering God's will that it denies itself. In our weakness, when natural strength has dwindled, we learn how to draw from the well of grace.

We have intentionally given ourselves to a lifetime pursuit of knowing him, and in doing so, we declare that the Lord is our most desirable treasure. He is our all. Our strength, comfort, wisdom, peace, and salvation. His blood cleanses us. His breath fills our lungs and awakens our souls. As we live in him, he uncovers all we need to prosper in every area. We remember that this holy and magnificent Lord has invited us to become one with him—intertwined within the very glory that created the heavens and the earth. The same splendor that has existed from before the beginning of time lives in us.

Today's Prayer

Lord, you are the single most crucial element of my life. To know and love you is my greatest joy. Thank you for extending the cup of fellowship and inviting me to drink from the well of grace that never runs dry. As I lose myself in you, I discover the peace that surpasses all reasoning. All distractions fade when I live inside the sufficiency of Christ and remember that you are enough. No, you are *more* than enough.

You are the crashing waves of hope upon my weary soul. The shield against fear and the joy that contradicts reasoning. When the enemy clouds my eyes with unbelief, you come in a blaze of glory that lights my way so I can see the truth with clarity. You teach me how to turn my attention so you alone hold my gaze.

I delight myself in you and your Word. Truth has become a banqueting table for my soul. And though my body may crave the foods I've set aside, my spirit feasts on the fullness of what you offer. I am satisfied by your love in a way I never knew possible.

Steps for Transformation

- What does God think about this fast? That may seem like an odd question, but I encourage you to ask him. One of the most incredible blessings of our lives is that we get to commune with this holy, magnificent King. And quite often, we assume we know what's on his heart without actually asking. When we esteem what he has to say more than what is on our prayer lists, we're putting love into action.

- Now ask the Lord for three more things he'd like to say. You may hear a single word or phrase, but whatever you hear, write it down. The subject matter isn't important. Then pray into what he said, asking him to expand it.

- Ask him for one or two things he's been teaching you in this season. Just sit and write what rises in your heart. You could go through previous journal entries and to find a theme. Once you've received something, write it down in the first person from the Lord. Example: *I've been teaching you the importance of starting each day in my presence.* The more comfortable you are hearing God for yourself, the easier it will be to share his heart with others.

And though my body may crave the foods I've set aside,
my spirit feasts on the fullness of what you offer.
I am satisfied by your love in a way I never knew possible.

Scripture to Ponder

The fountain of life flows from you to satisfy me.
In your light of holiness we receive the light of revelation.

PSALM 36:9

How he satisfies the souls of thirsty ones
and fills the hungry with goodness!

PSALM 107:9

Find your delight and true pleasure in Yahweh,
and he will give you what you desire the most.

PSALM 37:4

DAY 28

Rising to the Surface

Trials have a way of peeling back the layers of our faith to expose beliefs whose roots are not securely grounded and established in the Lord. They cause impurities to rise to the top so we can see what has been hiding beneath—doubt, impatience, selfishness, fear, and control that have been secretly raging against our freedom in Christ. We don't enjoy these seasons, but they can be blessings in disguise if we don't ignore what's rising to the surface of our souls.

Fasting has a similar effect. When we devote ourselves to times of fasting and prayer, we're inviting the Lord to reveal attitudes, impure motives, and other sins or strongholds so we can be cleansed and set free. We're choosing to face these issues with the Lord, instead of waiting for trials to force us to take notice of what's in our hearts. When you notice an attitude, a surge of anxiety, a reaction of frustration, or any of the myriad of ways the flesh reacts to hunger, don't brush them aside. They're rising as answers to prayer. This is your invitation to acknowledge areas that need healing or that you should lay at his feet in surrender.

Father, shine the light of your glory into the areas I've yet to face. I'm not afraid of seeing what you already know is there. Freedom is a gift that comes through your hands, but only if I'm willing to accept it. I'm willing, Lord. I want to be free in the depths of my soul, to experience your glory in every part of my being, to worship you without hindrance or distraction. I want to know you, to hear you—to be yours completely.

I will not pretend that all is well when it isn't. I will not excuse iniquity or put on airs of perfection. I want to walk before you with a clean heart and a posture of humble dependence. I want the truth that only you can reveal. That's why I've chosen to set myself aside to pursue you, to stop focusing on myself and instead come into your presence where darkness cannot hide. Bathe me in the light of your deliverance, and may the cleansing flow of mercy drench every part. Let conviction fall upon my heart, leaving me wonderfully undone before the throne of grace.

Steps for Transformation

- If you've been triggered emotionally during this fast, don't run from it. Write down what negative characteristics have been rising through words, actions, or attitudes (impatience, fear, or a multitude of other things). Ask the Lord to show you these sins from his perspective. In humility, ask him to forgive you and to give you the grace to separate yourself from them. Invite him to heal the places that need his touch. Be encouraged; the Holy Spirit won't let you see what cannot be changed. If he's exposing these things, it is because it's time to get free.

- If this fast hasn't triggered you, that's great! It's a perfect time to ask the Lord to uncover the areas where he wants you to grow or where he is calling you into a deeper relationship with him. With journal in hand, quiet yourself before the Lord and wait for him to speak. You're not trying to find something wrong. You're merely opening yourself for God to show where he is drawing you into a more powerful, more consecrated way of living. God has promised that you will continually grow from one level of glory to the next (see 2 Corinthians 3:18).

> *Bathe me in the light of your deliverance, and may the cleansing flow of mercy drench every part.*

Scripture to Ponder

Keep creating in me a clean heart.
Fill me with pure thoughts and holy desires,
ready to please you.

PSALM 51:10

Teach me more about you,
how you work and how you move,
so that I can walk onward in your truth
until everything within me brings honor to your name.

PSALM 86:11

God made the only one who did not know sin to become sin for us, so that we might become the righteousness of God through our union with him.

2 CORINTHIANS 5:21

DAY 29

Facing Truth

One endearing aspect of our relationship with the Lord is the way he corrects us. Conviction carries the tender love of our Father, which softens the heart and stirs a yearning for purity. At some point, most of us will come face-to-face with the uncomfortable revelation of self-power working in our lives. Where there is an inability to trust the Lord patiently, we often push to make things happen. Usually, this manifests in anxiety, fear, and taking into our own hands matters that are best left in his.

There is no grace when we strive to do things in our strength, and it reveals a lack of trust in the Lord. This unveiling of truth strips us of excuses but also invites us to be honest about how much we believe in his love. God wants us to see the ugliness of self-effort and its ties to fear so that we will crucify it. It is only through a deeper revelation of his love that fear will yield. Fear pushes us to act, but love allows us to wait patiently—to rest, to trust God's leading, and to be fully convinced that without him, we can do nothing. With love, we can acknowledge our weaknesses and invite him to be our strength.

Today's Prayer

Father, be my strength today. I've spent too much time trying to make things happen outside of your grace. I've taken on projects and have often run ahead of you, hoping you'd catch up. I've asked you to bless the work of my hands even when I neglected to consult you and seek your wisdom from the beginning. At times my heart and actions have been at odds. I've strived for what I thought would make me happy and divided my affections. Forgive me.

Thank you for being patient and merciful when I try to do things in my own strength. For holding me in my weakness and whispering words of grace. In impatience, I scooped up the surrendered heart I once offered to you. But I lay it down again, holding nothing back. In humility and wholehearted dependence, I confess my stubbornness and pride. I want to walk in the light of your presence, wholly submitted to you. I commit myself to do things your way, following the path paved with grace. I don't want to do life—any of it—on my own anymore.

Steps for Transformation

- When our eyes are on ourselves, they're not on the Lord. When we're consumed with what isn't going right, fear may creep in and coax us to take control. Fear is debilitating. The solution is to return our focus to the Lord. Today, let's behold perfect love that drives out fear. Start at the place where love conquered all. Go to the cross. See Jesus there. See the price of love. Reflect on the power of that moment and the glory that was to come. Ask for a fresh revelation of the cross. Don't rush. Look at him. Look at what he did for *you*. Before resurrection, there is death. This was true for Jesus, and it's true for you. It's time to take up your cross and follow him (see Matthew 16:24), to crucify every deed of the flesh and all desires that don't reflect his.

- Now see the victory of the cross. It is a place where suffering becomes joyful and immeasurably beautiful. No sacrifice is ever wasted. What the enemy means for harm, God uses for good. Each time you surrender, you are stepping into victory.

> *In impatience, I scooped up the surrendered heart I once offered to you. But I lay it down again, holding nothing back.*

Scripture to Ponder

My old identity has been co-crucified with Christ and no longer lives. And now the essence of this new life is no longer mine, for the Anointed One lives his life through me—we live in union as one! My new life is empowered by the faith of the Son of God who loves me so much that he gave himself for me, dispensing his life into mine!

GALATIANS 2:20

Jesus said to all of his followers, "If you truly desire to be my disciple, you must disown your life completely, embrace my 'cross' as your own, and surrender to my ways."

LUKE 9:23

Here's what I've learned through it all:
Don't give up; don't be impatient;
be entwined as one with the Lord.
Be brave and courageous, and never lose hope.
Yes, keep on waiting—for he will never disappoint you!

PSALM 27:14

DAY 30

He Has Prepared a Feast

As we come before the Lord, emptied of self, broken, and poured out before him like Mary Magdalene, we're in the perfect position to be filled. This choice to fast and seek his face is a declaration of our dependence upon him more than our need for food. We sit at his table of fellowship and, with empty stomachs, feast at his table. He pours out his love in lavish measure, and we drink our fill. He is the source of all we need.

We are the bride who is enthralled with her Beloved. We fast, not because we crave the approval of man, but because we yearn for holy intimacy without distractions. We long for Jesus, the Bread of Life. He is our sustenance. The One whose grace enables us to seek him with untainted desire. He completes us. Fills us with the abundance of who he is, so we lack nothing—though we've yielded everything. In him, we are fully alive. Thriving. Healthy in our spirit, soul, and body. Blessed beyond measure, simply by being in his arms. All other pursuits, even the loftiest dreams of our hearts, fail in comparison to the joy of knowing him.

Lord, you are my provision and great reward. My sustainer, comforter, and deliverer. It is my joy to feel the grip of hunger because it reminds me to feast on you, the Bread of Life. I love being reminded of my need for you. It is an honor to recognize my frailty. Weakness is a blessing that causes me to depend on you, to look to you, and to accept the strength that can only come from you.

Thank you for your grace during this fast. For stirring a most profound hunger that can only be satisfied by the substance of your love. Thank you for meeting with me and inviting me to draw closer. As I deny my flesh, you're teaching me to tap into the source of life that perfects me. You inspire me to laugh when all hell tempts me to doubt. How could I ever question your glory teeming within me? It is awakening a spiritual appetite that causes all other pursuits to fade into the distance. It is a mystery how my decision to suffer hunger invites the fullness of your Spirit. So fill me, Lord, as I separate myself unto you and dine at your table of fellowship.

Steps for Transformation

- During a fast, it's normal to experience cravings, feel hunger, or be tempted to quit. Instead of yielding to the heaviness of these things, rise above them. Use them as catapults to propel you straight into the glorious presence of God. Every time the hardship of fasting touches you, close your eyes and whisper his name in the silence of your heart. Engage with God's ever-present love. Lavish him with words of devotion, thanksgiving, and commitment. Let every craving be a reminder of how much more you desire him.

- As you learn to turn to the Lord in each temptation, it becomes easier to shake off the distraction. You get stronger when you depend on his sustaining grace. Drink of his love today and allow it to be your constant delight. Soon, fasting will become a joy. When you stop focusing on what you're depriving yourself of and continuously meditate on the glory of God filling you, being around food or the smell of your favorite dish won't faze you.

> *Lord, thank you for stirring a most profound hunger that can only be satisfied by the substance of your love.*

Scriptures to Ponder

Jesus said to them, "I am the Bread of Life.
Come every day to me and you will never be hungry.
Believe in me and you will never be thirsty."

JOHN 6:35

Our own completeness is now found in him. We are completely
filled with God as Christ's fullness overflows within us. He is the
Head of every kingdom and authority in the universe!

COLOSSIANS 2:10

I'm not defeated by my weakness, but delighted! For when I feel my
weakness and endure mistreatment—when I'm surrounded with
troubles on every side and face persecution because of my love for
Christ—I am made yet stronger. For my weakness becomes a portal
to God's power.

2 CORINTHIANS 12:10

DAY 31

Time

Busyness is among the greatest oppositions to a lifestyle of holy intimacy. Our need to accomplish as much as possible during a twenty-four-hour period forces us to rush. With a checklist in hand, we push aside meaningful encounters with the Lord in exchange for a hurried one-sided chat. We grab a verse to snack on as we run about while neglecting the feast that's been set before us.

This fast isn't a quick fix. It is an invitation to a lifestyle change. A reminder that we, the bride, were created to rest with the Lord in the chambers of his presence. Here, in the safety of his arms, we receive direction, wisdom, and peace for our day and the situations we'll face. We're refreshed and invigorated—his tenderness fanning our hearts with a second wind. As we prioritize our relationship with him and position ourselves to hear, to see, and to behold him, it's easier to maintain that posture throughout the day. We are strengthened by stillness. The fire of his love ignites our faith. And when first-love intimacy is our abiding place, it can be found in the driest of desert seasons.

Father, our divine relationship began because of your mercy and grace. You drew me out of darkness and welcomed me into your glorious light. When you whispered your love and awakened my heart, I responded. I stopped what I was doing and gave myself to you. And in the warmth of your embrace, it seemed time stood still. You washed me in the cleansing waters of love and wrapped me in garments of righteousness. We became one when love set me free.

What you initiated by your Spirit I cannot maintain by my fleshly efforts. I cannot work to earn your approval. Fasting is not a badge I can wear. Nothing I do will ever make me holy. But I can choose to remember your gift of love. I can honor you by responding to your gentle tug upon my heart. I can pause—again and again—and set my gaze on you. It was in the quiet of your presence that my life turned around, and it is here that my surrendered heart must remain. Forgive me for forsaking stillness, Lord. Thank you for revealing yourself again. Time with you is my delight.

Steps for Transformation

- What has the Lord been speaking to you during this fast? Has there been a recurring theme? What verses have come alive? What have you sensed the most when you're in his presence? For example, peace, joy, overwhelming love, a lifting of heaviness, etc. Be sure to journal everything you've sensed coming from the Lord during this time. God has been inviting many into a lifestyle change that isn't forced by outward circumstances. He has lovingly pointed out areas that need to change so you can enjoy the many blessings he has for you. Honor him by pondering everything he's shown you.

- I also want to encourage you. Over the years, almost every fast has left a holy mark on my heart. Even if I didn't realize it at the time and even in fasts that felt void of any real sense of breakthrough or divine encounter, something always shifted in me. Sometimes you'll sense it during the fast and other times not until afterward, but rest assured—if your attention has been on him—the Lord is doing a beautiful and mysterious work in you.

> *We became one*
> *when love set me free.*

Scripture to Ponder

Make your life a prayer.

1 Thessalonians 5:17

May the God of peace and harmony set you apart, making you completely holy. And may your entire being—spirit, soul, and body—be kept completely flawless in the appearing of our Lord Jesus, the Anointed One. The one who calls you by name is trustworthy and will thoroughly complete his work in you.

1 Thessalonians 5:23–24

Do the riches of his extraordinary kindness make you take him for granted and despise him? Haven't you experienced how kind and understanding he has been to you? Don't mistake his tolerance for acceptance. Do you realize that all the wealth of his extravagant kindness is meant to melt your heart and lead you into repentance?

Romans 2:4

DAY 32

Unbroken Fellowship

In prayer, God's presence is our aim. It is here that we connect with him. We seek his presence, search his wisdom, and listen as he shares. From a posture of worship, we lavish the Lord with our love. We pour out the oil of longing and bless him with our absolute surrender and sincere devotion. In these set apart times, we experience the beauty of communion with the One who loves us, unceasingly. But this divine connection isn't meant to be interrupted.

You were created to live in unbroken fellowship with your heavenly Father. Your time alone with him gives you a glimpse of what life in the spirit can be like, every moment of every day. Let this fast stir a desire for uninterrupted interaction between you and the Lord. Consider this his invitation to a more profound way of living that's centered around him. Ask God to be your everything and to ignite a desire for him that never dims. Then pay attention as he gently taps on the door of your heart throughout the day and answer the call by turning into his presence. Do this over and over again, until his presence becomes your place of continual abiding.

Today's Prayer

Father, I want more than visitations of your glory. I want to abide in the reality of your love forever, to know your heart every moment, and to be keenly aware of your desire. I want to live constantly aware of how near you are and to awaken that awareness in others. I long to feel the sweetness of your grace as I surrender every selfish ambition and to walk with confidence as I follow your voice.

Lord, reveal the distractions in my life that entice me to look away from you. Give me singleness of heart—the grace to stay focused on you at all times, no matter what's happening around me. Let the fires of holy love incinerate every mindset that doesn't lead to you. Demolish the obstacles of doubt and fear. Lift the veils of self that blur my vision and cause me to stumble. Take my hand and pull me close—I'm not satisfied with the touch of yesterday's encounter. Your Spirit is beckoning me closer, and my heart responds with cries of love.

Steps for Transformation

- Sometimes we make spiritual matters more complicated than God intends them to be. Our Father created us to have fellowship with him. Jesus has paid the price, and his Spirit lives inside of us. He has made it easy to live in communion with him. So, how do we do that on a practical level? It is an internal posture of the heart. Even when we aren't asking him a question or telling him something specific, we maintain a constant awareness of God. We can work or play and still have a sense of his presence all around us. Though at times we may lose consciousness of him, we know he hasn't left, and it becomes effortless to reengage. When we set the affections of our hearts upon him, our life becomes a prayer.

- The presence of the Lord can be just as real to you during your set apart prayer time as it is while you're busy doing other things. Today, let his presence be your continual feast. See how often you can turn your attention to him. As your heart remains engaged, you'll be surprised how easy it is to share his heart with others.

> *Take my hand and pull me close—I'm not satisfied with the touch of yesterday's encounter.*

Scripture to Ponder

You must catch the troubling foxes,
those sly little foxes that hinder our relationship.
For they raid our budding vineyard of love
to ruin what I've planted within you.
Will you catch them and remove them for me?
We will do it together.

SONG OF SONGS 2:15

Draw me into your heart.
We will run away together into the king's cloud-filled chamber.
The Chorus of Friends
We will remember your love, rejoicing and delighting in you,
celebrating your every kiss as better than wine.
No wonder righteousness adores you!

SONG OF SONGS 1:4

I'm standing at the door, knocking. If your heart is open to hear my
voice and you open the door within, I will come in to you and feast
with you, and you will feast with me.

REVELATION 3:20

DAY 33

Sensing the Shift

There is a point in time, a divine juncture when everything begins to turn in our favor. We may not see the physical manifestation yet, but we sense it. It seems as if a gentle breeze from heaven is blowing upon our souls—awakening us to the dawning of a new season. God's grace has led us here. His merciful heart has heard our cry. Now we stand at the threshold of blessings more glorious than we imagined. It is up to us to cross over.

The most glorious breakthroughs are just on the other side of our agreement. We may feel our faith being stirred like waters by the wind, but it's up to us to dive in. When we begin to experience excitement for what's coming, we must connect our faith. Fasting often precedes a shift in our lives. We often sense breakthrough in our spirit before we see it in the natural. When this happens, we don't need to analyze what's happening or try to find ways to speed up the process. We simply need to rest in a posture of trust. All God is looking for is our agreement—for the cry of surrender that rises from our heart.

Father, I'm gripped by joy unspeakable. Though I don't see the full manifestation of what's to come, it seems as if I'm already there in the spirit. I have such anticipation! Thank you for reviving my faith. Thank you for reminding me that your goodness is limitless. You are taking me from glory to glory, always leading me closer to you, where nothing hinders my vision.

With you, life is a wonderful journey. I'll leave the details in your capable hands, trusting you to lead the way and clear a path for me to follow. There is always something new to discover when my eyes are on you and I'm not distracted. My spirit and soul are invigorated. Holy longing has led me to you. You contain the answers I've been searching for. Here in the beauty of your presence, doubt and unbelief cannot find me. I am safe. I am yours. I am standing at the edge of breakthrough, ready to dive into the waters of your love where I am made whole.

Steps for Transformation

- When we sense the coming shift and faith gets stirred, we need to guard our hearts so that we don't become anxious in waiting. We may be tempted to tune out of the season we're in before it's time. As people who hear the Lord, it's crucial to not only agree with what he shows us but also trust his timing. For now, stay focused on what is in your hands.

- If you sense God is launching you into something new, keep your thoughts on him. Trust the Lord to reveal the details when you need them. Remain surrendered to his will; he will lead you. Don't overthink, reason, or analyze. If you have been, find your peace and put every concern on the altar. Ask yourself if you've made peace with God's timing. If not, surrender your timetable to the Lord.

- Sometimes we know exactly what's coming, and other times, we don't have a clue. When anticipation is coupled with mystery, take comfort—the Lord is encouraging your faith. It's okay not to understand what he's doing. Like a loving parent getting everything ready for Christmas morning, the Father is preparing his blessings for you.

> *You are taking me from glory to glory,*
> *always leading me closer to you,*
> *where nothing hinders my vision.*

Scripture to Ponder

As you wait for the reality of what I am creating,
be filled with joy and unending gladness!
Look! I am ready to create Jerusalem
as a source of sheer joy,
and her people, an absolute delight!

ISAIAH 65:18

My heart and soul explode with joy—full of glory!
Even my body will rest confident and secure.

PSALM 16:9

Yahweh is my strength and my wraparound shield.
When I fully trust in you, help is on the way.
I jump for joy and burst forth with ecstatic, passionate praise!
I will sing songs of what you mean to me!

PSALM 28:7

DAY 34

Beholding Him Releases Wisdom

It's easy to get distracted. All day long, worldly distractions lure us away from the simplicity of beholding the Lord. Even during a fast, when we intend to seek him more, we can lose focus. Trials and disappointments dangle in front of us as if they're something worth contemplating, and our mind takes the bait. Once we fixate on a problem, our entire being can become consumed, almost tormented, by the soul's incessant banter. Hours, sometimes days go by before we realize how much time and energy we've wasted brooding over a problem. But natural wisdom can only take us so far.

We will not discover the mind of Christ in an atmosphere of anxiety. To access his magnificent wisdom, we first have to get out of our heads and tap into his heart. We must yield to peace because when we do, it's easier to know his will. The revelation of his desire only comes after we lay our analyzing, our need for control, and our constant thinking and talking about our problems on the altar. If this fast changes anything in us, let it be that we're becoming absolutely convinced of God's love. We're learning that beholding the Lord, and *keeping* our focus on him, changes everything.

Today's Prayer

Lord, when I step outside of the awareness of your presence, I get stuck in my head. Tempted to figure things out on my own, I become weighted with burdens I'm not meant to carry. Decisions, commitments, and stresses steal my peace, but only when I take my eyes off you. Only when I allow my mind to go where it shouldn't. Forgive me for sacrificing my peace on the altar of self-power, where I try to force a solution without you. Come and lead me by your Spirit as I turn my heart to you again.

Only your love is powerful enough to keep me in perfect peace. I can't even fix my mind on you without your enabling grace. And when questions swirl, compelling me to take charge, remind me to submit my will to you. In the place of trust, I can wait for your answer with a peaceful heart. You have promised to guide me with your eyes, so instead of staring at my problem, I'll gaze upon you. Enjoying the powerful simplicity of beholding you, no matter what comes, is a gift I choose to accept. You *are* the peace that passes understanding.

Steps for Transformation

- What are you thinking about? I suggest writing down the subjects that run through your mind on a continual basis. Make a list of one-word concerns. For example, if you're worried about someone, write that person's name. If health or finances are causing anxiety, write "health" or "finances." Whatever is occupying more space in your heart than you know is healthy, write it down. Then ask the Lord for one or two promises from his Word to write next to those items.

- Spend time pondering those verses throughout the day. Every time a burden tries to steal your attention, speak the Word and allow the Holy Spirit to massage it into your heart. Ask him to tell you exactly what he wants you to glean from the passages and expect that promise to come alive inside of you.

- If your mind is glued to a problem, forcing yourself to stop thinking about it may be difficult. There's much more grace in thinking about something else (see Philippians 4:8). By meditating on God's Word, love, and faithfulness, peace will begin to heal the scars of trauma and worry.

> *You have promised to guide me with your eyes,*
> *so instead of staring at my problem,*
> *I'll gaze upon you.*

Scripture to Ponder

I hear the Lord saying, "I will stay close to you,
instructing and guiding you along the pathway for your life.
I will advise you along the way
and lead you forth with my eyes as your guide."

PSALM 32:8–9

Above all, constantly seek God's kingdom and his righteousness,
then all these less important things will be given to you abundantly.
Refuse to worry about tomorrow, but deal with each challenge that
comes your way, one day at a time. Tomorrow will take care of itself.

MATTHEW 6:33

Because I set you, Yahweh, always close to me,
my confidence will never be weakened,
for I experience your wraparound presence every moment.

PSALM 16:8

DAY 35

Until Your Soul Sings Again

The Lord's love for you is immeasurably intense and deeply personal. He didn't prompt you to do this fast because he was frustrated with you. He wooed you close and stirred your heart because he longs for you to experience true love in a deeper measure. The mystery of holy union with him is your destiny. It is the reward of Christ's suffering. You are the gift Jesus gave his life to obtain. You are the object of his affection.

Allow the revelation of God's love to permeate you today. Close your eyes to the distractions that have been bombarding you and set your gaze upon the Lord. Feel love's refreshing breeze, and it will cause your spirit to soar. He sees you, beloved. He hears you. He knows what's on your heart; now it's time to listen to what's on his. You will find the answers you need in his presence, so don't resist. Lean in. Be still and rest with him. You don't have to strive. You only need to trust and enjoy this magnificent gift of love. He *is* the breakthrough. He *is* the peace that stills your soul. Stay here, wrapped in his glorious love, until your soul sings again.

Lord, you have torn the veil between us. Now nothing can hinder me from running into your presence and drinking deeply from the fountain that never runs dry. Saturate my dry ground. Flood my senses with the substance of your love, until it is all I feel, taste, hear, see, and smell. I want to be consumed by glory so that when I look in the mirror, all I see is you.

Deep within my veins I feel the fire in your eyes. Your love, power, and holiness are blazing through every cell. No one holds my heart the way you do. Make me wholly yours until every movement of my soul sings your praise and nothing else vies for my attention. I want to know you as you know me. I want every thought to bow before your majesty in holy surrender continuously. Lord, whisper mysteries of sacred love until every part of me responds. Your gentle hands have restored me and made me whole. Now I live face-to-face with the One whom my soul loves, and my life will echo your unending devotion.

Steps for Transformation

- The veil of separation has been torn. The blood of Jesus has made provision for you to be as close to him as you'd like. As a child of God, you are standing in his presence right now. Nothing is separating you from him. See Jesus before you. Walk right up to him and look into his eyes. What do you see? Purity, fire, compassion, righteousness, love? Yes! All of these things and more. Come as a child filled with curiosity and lock eyes with the One who calls you his poem and his masterpiece (Ephesians 2:10). As you gaze into those beautiful eyes, wait there. Don't rush. Expect to see varying aspects of his glory—more magnificent than you've ever seen before. Take note and allow the glorious revelation of his magnificent love to be your mediation today.

- Let love be your focus as you stand face-to-face with him *every day*. Each time you come, a shift is taking place within you. You cannot approach the Lord with an open heart and not receive something from him. May this fast shift you into an attitude of expectancy unlike anything you've ever known.

> *Lord, whisper mysteries of holy love*
> *until every part of me responds.*

Scripture to Ponder

I long to drink of you, O God,
to drink deeply from the streams of pleasure
flowing from your presence.
My longings overwhelm me for more of you!

PSALM 42:1

It is Christ's love that fuels our passion and holds us tightly, because
we are convinced that he has given his life for all of us. This means
all died with him, so that those who live should no longer live self-
absorbed lives but lives that are poured out for him—the one who
died for us and now lives again.

2 CORINTHIANS 5:14–15

My heart is on fire, boiling over with passion.
Bubbling up within me are these beautiful lyrics
as a lovely poem to be sung for the King.
Like a river bursting its banks, I'm overflowing with words,
spilling out into this sacred story.

PSALM 45:1

DAY 36

The Garden

The cries of loving worship springing up from the depths of your soul are beginning to set you free. God is transforming your wilderness into a resting place of bliss, where songs of love and trust flow effortlessly. As you set your heart on him, you're becoming his beautiful garden, blossoming with fragrant grace. Here, in the quiet of your soul, he meets with you, shares secrets, heals your heart, and empowers you for a life of victory.

You will never know the joys you were created for until you discover them *in him*. By stepping out of the landscape of everyday distraction and placing all of your attention on things lovely, pure, and true, you come alive. You will find yourself, your true identity, when he alone consumes you. You were created to love and be loved, to know Jesus as Savior, friend, and Lord, and to walk with him and grow into his likeness, hearing what only longing hearts can hear. So, never stop longing. Never cease to take these garden walks, inviting him to till the soil of your soul. Maintain the beauty of your inner sanctuary by surrendering to him day after day and nurturing your beautiful relationship.

Today's Prayer

Father, I turn my heart to you. Let's meet in our secret garden where your wraparound presence encloses me. Speak to me, hold me, heal me, and laugh with me. Sit and impart your wisdom. Root me and ground me in the soil of your love. Take my hand and lead me into encounters that change me from the inside out. Touch my mind and release spiritual understanding that sets others free. I want to be like you—to echo your heart and mirror your beauty, to be a vessel of this magnificent love.

What joy I've found in your presence! What sweet release. This is what I needed—just to be with you, to see the light and truth that emanate from your being, to remember that I am created in your image and that I am your delight. Here, in your presence, nothing else matters except giving myself without reservation. So, I hold nothing back from you. Let the deepest depths of our union be evident in everything I say and do. And may your glory blossom from within me until the fragrance of your love drips from every cell.

Steps for Transformation

- The more we see the Lord and spend time with him, the greater our desire to be like him, to know him, and to hold nothing back. As you soak in his love today, ask him if there are any areas in your life that you haven't completely surrendered. Are there any circumstances that you are trying to control instead of trusting him to work them out? Quiet yourself and listen. He will never condemn you or make you feel shame, but he will correct and give you the grace to change.

- The Lord thinks the best of you. He sees you differently than you see yourself. You are his treasure that he purchased with the price of sacred blood. When you see yourself the way he sees you, it releases encouragement and faith. Ask the Lord what he loves about you. The moment you hear the answer, write it down. Embrace the sweet, loving message you've heard from his heart.

- Now bless the Lord by telling him what you love about him.

> *May your glory blossom from within me*
> *until the fragrance of your love*
> *drips from every cell.*

Scripture to Ponder

Your inward life is now sprouting, bringing forth fruit.
What a beautiful paradise unfolds within you.
When I'm near you, I smell aromas of the finest spice,
for many clusters of my exquisite fruit
now grow within your inner garden.

SONG OF SONGS 4:13–14

I have gathered from your heart,
my equal, my bride,
I have gathered from my garden
all my sacred spices—even my myrrh.
I have tasted and enjoyed my wine within you.
I have tasted with pleasure my pure milk, my honeycomb,
which you yield to me.
I delight in gathering my sacred spice,
all the fruits of my life I have
gathered from within you, my paradise garden.
Come, all my friends—feast
upon my bride, all you revelers of my palace.

SONG OF SONGS 5:1

DAY 37

These Are His Gifts

The blazing colors of sunset cannot summarize the Lord's beauty nor the most majestic stars waltzing among the planets. The ocean waves and bellowing winds, in all their strength, are mere trinkets compared to his power. The brightness of the sun and moon are only reflections of his radiance. Yet all of these displays bring the glory of God close to us. They work together to make his love and power visible, tangible. They provide a taste of his magnificence.

During this fast, take the time to enjoy the beauty of nature. Sit on a sunny beach or in a shady park alone with him. Walk barefoot through the grass. Quietly gaze at the evening stars as he wraps you in the warmth of his love. Notice the breeze as it caresses your skin with his touch. Watch as the trees dance with the wind. Listen for the birds, cracks of thunder, or quivering waters at the lake's edge. Then remember—all of these wonders of earth and sky are given to you as demonstrations—samples of the wonders, joys, and mysteries of your loving Father. These gifts are for your enjoyment, but more importantly, they point you to their Creator. Pay attention to the beauty surrounding you. Each recognition is an opportunity to connect with him.

Today's Prayer

Lord, thank you for these brilliant displays of glory diffused throughout the world. For daily reminders of your thoughtfulness, attention, and care. For painting skies with me in mind and inviting me to dance with you upon an earth tone stage. As breathtaking as creation is, you are more beautiful still. The splendor streaming from your face seizes my attention and enraptures my soul. You are the light that has illuminated my life. Nature echoes your sound, but it is the melody of your voice that has captured my heart forever.

You alone are my joy. My refreshing breeze and faithful friend. You are colorful and surprising. Your whispers, as gentle as the snow. You are majestic and your glory incomprehensible, yet you daily make time for me—showering me with kisses of delight and drawing me near. Throughout this fast, you have reminded me of your ever-present, over-the-top love. Your generous gifts are scattered everywhere for me to find—treasures of your magnificent kindness. And now, I bow before you as nature plays our symphony of love.

Steps for Transformation

- Taking the cue from today's devotion, think about your favorite aspects of nature. Some of mine are sunrise and sunset, the ocean, mountains, and a starry sky. Each reminds me of the kindness, creative genius, and infinite power of our Father. This week, enjoy at least one of the aspects of nature that speak to you. As you do, ponder this: God is even more beautiful than all of these. He is so magnificent, diverse, and multi-dimensional that he must display himself in facets scattered throughout the entire world and through every person on the face of the earth.

- What aspect of himself is God revealing to you? Revelation 4:8–11 tells us that the living creatures and elders are continually undone by what they see when they look at him. Ponder what he's showing you about his character and write it down.

- As incomprehensible as it may seem, while God's glory enraptures us, *he* is also captivated by *us*. The Father sees *you* through rose-tinted lenses. He sees you perfect, whole, and complete in Christ. You, redeemed one, are what holds his attention. Let this truth take root in your heart today.

> *Nature echoes your sound,*
> *but it is the melody of your voice*
> *that has captured my heart forever.*

Scripture to Ponder

Lift up your eyes to the sky and see for yourself.
Who do you think created the cosmos?
He lit every shining star and formed every glowing galaxy,
and stationed them all where they belong.
He has numbered, counted, and given everyone a name.
They shine because of God's incredible power
and awesome might; not one fails to appear!

ISAIAH 40:26

God's splendor is a tale that is told,
written in the stars.
Space itself speaks his story
through the marvels of the heavens.
His truth is on tour in the starry vault of the sky,
showing his skill in creation's craftsmanship.
Each day gushes out its message to the next,
night by night whispering its knowledge to all—
without a sound, without a word, without a voice being heard,
yet all the world can hear its echo.
Everywhere its message goes out.

PSALM 19:1–4

DAY 38

Secrets

The Lord longs to reveal himself to humble, yearning hearts. He waits in the stillness—ready to share secrets with those who will listen. Today, he is extending the invitation to go deeper into his glory—to search out the treasures he's hidden for you to find, to believe that your Father is excited about sharing his heart with you. Step into the open doors of his chambers where only family can go. Take his hand as he leads you to sit beside him, then lean in, wait, and listen.

Stillness is the sanctuary of revelation, where answers land effortlessly upon yearning souls, and where joys previously unknown are graciously imparted. This fast is awakening a desire to know the Lord in ways you never knew possible. He's been waiting to escort you into this next level of glory where you can hear the secrets he's tucked away just for you. You are his beloved, his child, the one he has blessed with ears to hear and a heart to know. So go closer and closer still. His voice is a gift you are meant to unwrap every day.

Today's Prayer

Lord, I'm leaning in—my ear so close I imagine I can feel your breath. My heart is tuned in and quiet, choosing to listen, not speak. Yours is the voice I long to hear. Your whispers bring me hope. You are the peace that passes understanding. Your wisdom ignites faith in every circumstance. Your secrets delight my soul and make me come alive.

Sometimes I hear you through your words—your whispers transforming the way I think. Other times, I simply feel, sense, or inexplicably know. When images of love, power, faith, and purity dance through my imagination, I know they're snapshots of your desire. Other times, I open your Word, and truth flows out. It doesn't matter how you communicate; it only blesses me that you do. You're always speaking, but I'm just not always quiet enough to hear. Forgive me. Instead of striving to know your will, I'll rest and remember that you are the One who made it possible for me to come close. And during the times when I cannot seem to find your voice, I will sit in the wonder of your love. I will wait and enjoy you. I trust that you know how to speak to this heart that you created.

Steps for Transformation

- It's so vital that we remain aware of what the Lord is teaching us during this fast. Sometimes we get excited about an encounter but don't honor the Lord by processing the significance with him or allowing the lessons to reach our hearts. Like a cow that chews its food, digests, and then rechews later to get more nutrients out of it, we, too, must give every encounter, revelation, and lesson the attention it deserves.

- Regardless of the time of year, write the name of each month that has passed so far. Below it, list the people, events, and more that God has worked through to speak to you, convey his love, encourage you, and strengthen you. Take your time on this. Mentally walk through each month, remembering the events, conversations, and other actions that impacted you.

- Ponder each of these things and write down the lesson he was and still is teaching you.

- Do you see how, even in the smallest ways, he makes his love, care, and attention known to you? Take time now to pour out your words of gratefulness. Let him know how thankful you are for the ways he reaches out to you.

> *I trust that you know how to speak to this heart that you created.*

Scripture to Ponder

There's a private place reserved for
the devoted lovers of Yahweh,
where they sit near him and receive
the revelation-secrets of his promises.

PSALM 25:14

Stop imitating the ideals and opinions of the culture around you,
but be inwardly transformed by the Holy Spirit through a total
reformation of how you think. This will empower you to discern
God's will as you live a beautiful life, satisfying and perfect in his eyes.

ROMANS 12:2

Faith, then, is birthed in a heart that responds to God's anointed
utterance of the Anointed One.
Can it be that Israel hasn't heard the message?
No, they have heard it, for:
The voice has been heard throughout the world,
and its message has gone to the ends of the earth!

ROMANS 10:17–18

DAY 39

Breathe Again

Trying to make things happen in your strength is exhausting. Sometimes it isn't until you've come to the end of yourself that God steps in. Perhaps in your case, a fast for deeper intimacy isn't what you wanted. You wanted to storm the gates of hell, strategically plan your breakthrough, or to fast your way to the answers you need. Perhaps you thought you could get God's attention if you cried louder and proved your sincerity. Instead, he wooed you into the simplicity of love. He invited you to rest in his presence so that you can breathe again.

God wants to be your Father. He wants to give you the answers you need, but first, he wants to refresh you. The Lord called you to this fast so that you would remember how wonderful it is to live in the beauty of his love. And he wants you to believe in his love, once again. It's time to stop fighting for the breakthrough he's promised as if the pressure is on you to make it happen. An attitude of faith is powerful enough to move mountains. God hasn't forsaken you. He's just been waiting for you to let go. The posture of a believing heart is one of rest.

Father, thank you for stirring my heart to spend this time with you. Forgive me for any time I've searched for answers outside of you. For thinking that resting in your love couldn't possibly change anything because it was too easy. I repent for working myself into a frenzy and striving to obtain an ounce of improvement when you already offered me abundant breakthrough, free of charge.

Now I see that everything I need is found in you, and you hold nothing back when I believe in your love. I'm learning that your healing presence is all my weary soul requires and that rest is crucial. In this place of absolute surrender and unwavering trust, I experience peace beyond comprehension. You know exactly how to lead me through every season of life; you're often just waiting for me to be still enough to hear your directions. When I thoroughly let go and sink into your limitless love, I can breathe again. I can hope again. I can believe because you are my faithful, generous, and kind Father. Nothing can overwhelm me when I'm tucked away safely in your presence.

Steps for Transformation

- Remember what you wrote yesterday regarding the ways the Lord has been speaking and teaching you. Carry the awareness of his faithfulness, nearness, and ever-present love as you go about your day. If possible, practice one lesson for each part of the day. For example, if he's been talking to you about trust, spend the morning reminding yourself how he's proven his faithfulness to you. Perhaps he's been encouraging you to spend more time in the quiet of his presence. Spend the afternoon practicing contemplation. If he's been talking about the importance of meditating on his Word, spend the evening doing that.

- Hopefully, this fast has cracked the shell of worry, stress, and anxiety and brought you into a new level of peace. God wants peace to be your foundation, your new normal so that fear and worry feel foreign and unwelcome. If you're still struggling to find peace, stop. You don't have to fight for mental peace. It is found by completely resigning yourself to his care and drowning yourself in his love so every concern effortlessly rises to the surface where he scoops it up and carries it away.

> *You know exactly how to lead me through every season of life;*
> *you're often just waiting for me to be still enough*
> *to hear your directions.*

Scripture to Ponder

Now, Lord, do it again! Restore us to our former glory!
May streams of your refreshing flow over us
until our dry hearts are drenched again.

PSALM 126:4

His pleasure and passion is remaining true to the Word of "I AM,"
meditating day and night on the true revelation of light.
He will be standing firm like a flourishing tree
planted by God's design,
deeply rooted by the brooks of bliss,
bearing fruit in every season of his life.
He is never dry, never fainting,
ever blessed, ever prosperous.

PSALM 1:2–3

When you fast, don't let it be obvious, but instead, wash your
face and groom yourself and realize that your Father in the secret
place is the one who is watching all that you do in secret and will
continue to reward you.

MATTHEW 6:17–18

DAY 40

Every Day

On this final day of fasting, the One who was, is, and ever will be wants to remind you of his love and your place within it. It doesn't matter how long you fasted, if you did it perfectly, or got distracted. His love for you is unconditional and eternal. Every movement of your heart toward him has caught his attention. Not one tear of overflowing devotion has ever gone unnoticed. You are his chosen one—the one he moved heaven and earth to be with.

From this day forward, allow unconditional love to redefine the way you see yourself and the world around you. Submit your fears, stresses, and worries to the flames of his fiery passion. Invite the Lord to burn away lies that have hindered your ability to trust in this holy relationship. Swim in the deep rivers of his love so any thought contrary to his faithfulness will be drowned in glory. Saturate yourself in his presence until nothing matters more than to be with him. This is where you are called to live each day—in the place of absolute surrender, unwavering trust, and joyous wonder.

Today's Prayer

Lord, come and seal my heart with your holy fire. Set me aflame with longing for you that never grows dim. I want to know you, to see, hear, taste, smell, and touch the reality of heaven that fills my life. Consume me. Wash away the debris that has become stuck in my thinking and give me the mind of Christ. Let every thought lead to you.

Ignite me with love so powerful and tangible that it becomes like fire in my bones—intense and undeniable. You have awakened my heart to the beauty of life in your presence, and I never want to leave. Lord, hold me close and never let me wander—not even for a moment. Purify my motives so that honoring you, pleasing you, following your will, and loving you become my sole obsessions. This is where I want to live each day—in the beauty of your presence, beholding your eyes that blaze with fire for your bride. Wrap me in your arms until I become your living flame of glory so all the world will know the greatness of your love.

Steps for Transformation

- Though this is the last day of the fast, a lifestyle of holy intimacy with the Lord can continue every day. Think about what you have implemented. What changes have you made in the way you've been spending time with God? Have you been enjoying more quiet time? Reading and meditating on the Word or listening intentionally for his voice more? Take note of the positive changes you've made and implement them as a way of life.

- Remember, as you've sought his face and the sweetness of his fellowship, God's been working on your behalf. The sacrifice of the foods you love, social media, television, or whatever else you laid down has not gone unnoticed. Every movement of your heart toward him has caught his attention. The times you've worshiped and trusted instead of fearfully begging have served to grow your faith. Throughout the next week or possibly even further out, you may notice breakthrough and blessing coming in unexpected ways. Continue journaling what he's teaching you and how you're changing.

- Whenever you officially end your fast, I encourage you to take holy communion. At the end of this book, you'll find a prayer to lead you in this respect.

> *Set me aflame
> with longing for you
> that never grows dim.*

Scripture to Ponder

Even the strong and the wealthy grow weak and hungry,
but those who passionately pursue the Lord will never lack any
good thing.

PSALM 34:10

I have come to set the earth on fire,
and how I wish it were already ablaze
with fiery passion for God!

LUKE 12:49

Here is what the Lord has spoken to me:
"Because you loved me, delighted in me,
and have been loyal to my name,
I will greatly protect you."

PSALM 91:14

Ending the Fast with Communion

I cannot think of a better way to end a fast than by partaking of holy communion. When we take communion, we remember the sacrifice of love. We are honoring the price Jesus paid to cleanse us from sin so that we can be with him forever. We also remember the priceless gifts he has given us to enjoy on earth. Let's conclude this time of fasting by thanking him for all he has done.

Grab a cracker or a small portion of bread and a bit of juice, read the verse below, and let's take communion together.

The same night in which he was handed over, he took bread and gave thanks. Then he distributed it to the disciples and said, "Take it and eat your fill. It is my body, which is given for you. Do this to remember me." He did the same with the cup of wine after supper and said, "This cup seals the new covenant with my blood. Drink it—and whenever you drink this, do it to remember me."

1 Corinthians 11:23–25

Let's Pray

Lord, I want to finish this fast by honoring you.

Thank you for this bread, a symbol of your body, which was beaten and broken for me. I'm so grateful that because of your great love for me, you willingly endured the agony and humiliation on my behalf. You took my sin on the cross so that nothing could separate us. Resurrection power has come into my life because of your death. The arms that once spread wide have drawn me close. You are my example of perfect and unselfish love. Thank you for dying for me. All I can do is cry, *Holy, holy, holy*, joining the angels in their declaration that has no end. I take this bread now, in remembrance of you.

Jesus, I hold the cup before you and acknowledge the power of your blood. It's hard to believe that I was the joy set before you. You endured the cross and suffered the shame for me. Salvation, healing, and virtue surge into my life today because of this precious blood. Thank you. The place of torture and suffering has become the most treasured proof of pure and unselfish love. Wash me. Cleanse me. Reveal anything in my life that doesn't reflect your beauty. Lord, seal the work you're doing in my heart with your blood. I humble myself before you and acknowledge my need for you, my Savior. As I drink this cup, I remember the price you paid for my redemption. Jesus, I love you, and I declare that I am yours forever.

Amen.

About the Author

Gretchen Rodriguez authored several devotionals alongside Brian Simmons to accompany The Passion Translation. Her heart burns with one main message: intimacy with Jesus and discovering the reality of his presence. She and her husband invested nine years as missionaries in Puerto Rico, along with their three daughters, and now make Redding, California, their home. For more about Gretchen, see her website: gretchenrodriguez.com.